THE GREAT STATE OF MAINE
BEER BOOK

"Cheers!

Will Anderson

Street Scene On A Summer Afternoon

Portland, Maine
August 1995

A Lively and Engaging Look

at Maine's Brewing Past and Present

THE GREAT STATE OF MAINE

BEER BOOK

by WILL ANDERSON

Anderson & Sons' Publishing Co.

7 Bramhall Terrace

Portland, Maine 04103

Library of Congress Catalogue Card Number 96-83097

Will Anderson 1940-
1. Popular Culture 2. Maine

ISBN 0-9601056-8-9

Studio photography by A. & J. DuBois Commercial Photography, Lewiston, Maine
Field photography by Ace Photog Studios, Portland, Maine
Typeset and printed by Spectrum Printing and Graphics, Auburn, Maine
Printed on 80lb. Somerset Gloss Recycled, S.D. Warren Co., Skowhegan, Maine

Cover graphics, clockwise – more or less – from upper left:
Label design, 1996, Sea Dog Brewing Co., Bangor and Camden
Ad, 1869, P. McGlinchy, Portland
Label design, 1996, Gritty McDuff's, Freeport and Portland
Label design, 1996, Bar Harbor Brewing Co., Bar Harbor
Photo, October 1995, Shipyard Brewing Co., Portland
Headline, July 1, 1933, *Waterville Morning Sentinel*, Waterville
Ad, July 1933, *The Bath Daily Times*, Bath
Photo, November 1995, waitress Kelly Drake serves up a pint, Theo's Restaurant/Sugarloaf Brewing Co., Carrabassett Valley
Photo, November 1995, Maine Coast Brewing Co., Bar Harbor
Coaster, 1996, Sunday River Brewing Co., Bethel
Photo, March 1988, left to right, Maine brewing pioneers Alan Pugsley, Karen Geary, David Geary, Portland

Table of Contents

Acknowledgements

**Enough people to fill a fair-sized brewpub or two
were good enough to help me as I researched and wrote
THE GREAT STATE OF MAINE BEER BOOK.
I'd like to especially thank:**

Laura Albans, Bangor Historical Society, Bangor   Avis Armstrong, Caribou   Valdine Atwood, Machias

Kathie Barrie, Portland Public Library, Portland   Dave Beckelman, Colonial Distributors, Waterville

Thomas C. Bennett, Portland Public Library, Portland   Sandi Brown-Eustis, Mechanic Falls Public Library, Mechanic Falls

Mara Buck, Windsor   Carmine Castaldo, National Distributors, South Portland

Gwen Campbell, Canton Historical Society, Canton   Jack Chisholm, McArthur Public Library, Biddeford

Marilyn Clark, Turner Memorial Library, Presque Isle   Donald R. Close, Portland Public Library, Portland

Joan Conroy, McArthur Public Library, Biddeford

Anne Cough, Maine State Library, Augusta   Jim Cyr, Turner Memorial Library, Presque Isle

Paul D'Alessandro, Portland Public Library, Portland   Al Diamon, Portland

Linda Fairfield, Rockland Public Library, Rockland   Jody Farra, Shenandoah, Pa.

Tom Gaffney, Portland Public Library, Portland   Matthew A. Hein, The Beer Institute, Washington, D.C.

Tom Hug, Lorain, Ohio   Judi Inchauteguiz, Skowhegan House of History, Skowhegan

Robert Jaeger, National Ass'n. of Breweriana Advertising, Wauwatosa, Wisc.   Jill Jakeman, Dyer Library, Saco

Roger Johnson, Biddeford-Saco Chamber of Commerce, Biddeford   William B. Jordan, Jr., Portland

Mary Lou Kelley, Portland Public Library, Portland   Dave Kesel, D.L. Geary Brewing Co., Portland

Karen Ketover, Walker Memorial Library, Westbrook   Sarah Korn, Camden Public Library, Camden

Molly Larson, Bangor Public Library, Bangor   Stuart Martin, Rumford Point

Susan Maxsimic, Bangor Public Library, Bangor   Frances McGlinchey, Gorham

Anna McGrath, University of Maine, Presque Isle   Barbara McIntosh, *Lewiston Sun-Journal*, Lewiston

Al McPherson, Pine Tree Beverage, Augusta   Ernie Oest, Port Jefferson Station, N.Y.   Ken Ostrow, Newton, Mass.

Sharon Packer, Auburn   Edie Perry, Allen Management Co., Bangor

Bob Pickett, North Berwick   Rick Poore, Standish   Dale Rand, Portland   Frances Raye, Perry

Roberta Richards, Strong   Charles Richelieu, Bath Historical Society, Bath

Betty Robinson, Thomaston Historical Society, Thomaston   Diana Robson, Camden Public Library, Camden

Steve Ross, Cumberland & York Distributors, Portland   Irene S. Russak, Allen Management Co., Bangor

Susan Sager, Bangor Historical Society, Bangor   Dick Shaw, *Bangor Daily News*, Bangor

Richard Sibley, Waterville Public Library, Waterville   Virginia Smith, Buckfield Historical Society, Buckfield

Pauline M. Sodermark, Corinth Historical Society, East Corinth   John Stanley, Durham, N.C.

Arlene Strahan, City of Waterville, Waterville   Jane Thompson, Carroll

Dale Van Wieren, East Coast Breweriana Ass'n., West Point, Pa.

Claire Ward, Lewiston Public Library, Lewiston   Don Weston, Winterport

Rita Wormwood, Maine State Library, Augusta

Plus I'd like to extend **special thanks** to Gil Strait and Morgan Mosher of Spectrum Printing & Graphics for their unceasing care and concern all along the way as **THE GREAT STATE OF MAINE BEER BOOK** progressed from manuscript and raw dummy to full-fledged book.

Preface

Did brewing have a life in Maine before David Geary arrived on the scene with his pioneering Geary's Pale Ale in 1986? The answer, surprisingly, is "yes." In fact, David – and the brewing cohorts who have followed – is descended from a rather large array of Mainers who have done their best to turn malt and water and hops into that magic beverage known as beer.

THE GREAT STATE OF MAINE BEER BOOK tells the tale of these early Maine brewing mavens in the section I've so cleverly entitled Part I = Old Brewers. The years where Maine and the nation were "dry" – but where rumrunning abounded – is entitled Part II = No Brewers. You can probably guess what I've entitled the last section. It's Part III = New Brewers. It's the part, of course, that includes all the marvelous brews and brewers that we are fortunate to have in Maine today. They brew some great stuff!

I've very much enjoyed researching and writing each section. I hope you have as much enjoyment reading it.

Will Anderson

Portland, Maine
May 14, 1996

This book is very lovingly dedicated to a truly
wonderful Mainer – my wife, Catherine – without
whose help and encouragement THE GREAT
STATE OF MAINE BEER BOOK would most likely
just be THE GOOD STATE OF MAINE BEER
BOOK.

Part I = Old Brewers

When I began the research for this part of THE GREAT STATE OF MAINE BEER BOOK - the section on the state's old-time commercial brewers - I expected to unearth very few candidates. Possibly eight or ten or so: three or four in Portland, a couple in Lewiston/Auburn, a couple in Bangor/Brewer, maybe one or two elsewhere. Instead I discovered that there were scores of candidates, with some even located in pretty wild and crazy places like Canton and East Corinth and Machias and Winterport. And "candidate" is the right word, because with quite a few of them it is nigh on to impossible to confirm that what they made was real beer - ale or lager or small beer (a relatively low alcohol brew meant to be consumed shortly after having been brewed) - as opposed to hop beer, root beer, spruce beer, or tonic beer, all of which are basically soft drinks. Or, in a number of other cases, to confirm that what is thought to have been a brewery even ever existed.

Researching old-time brewers, in Maine anyway, is not unlike going to bat against Roger Clemens. Occasionally you get a scratch hit. Occasionally you get a solid hit. Mostly you strike out. That's because there is no central information source: no computer printout of old-time Maine brewers; no book entitled WHO WAS WHO IN VACATIONLAND BREW. And Augusta's records re beer and alcohol go back only to 1933. Brewers, in short, were not a big deal. There were no television interviews. No radio talk shows. The "media" was the newspapers, which were often as much a vehicle for gossip and advertising as for news. But, then again, a brewery opening or closing wasn't considered news anyway. And most of Maine's pioneer brewers were so very small that they didn't care to advertise. Even if they did care to, many a newspaper publisher of the day was a temperance advocate and wouldn't accept alcoholic beverage advertising or anything akin to it.

Through a patchwork of various state directories, city directories, local histories, historical society and library personnel, census data, and quite possibly a solid mile of period newspapers on file on microfilm, however, I believe I have succeeded in rounding up the cast of Maine's brewing fraternity of yesteryear. Have I missed a few? Probably. Have I included a few who really didn't brew beer as we know it or anything that approximates it? Probably. My motto has been: "When in doubt, do not leave a possible brewer out." As a result, it's likely that some of those included in the cast didn't actually exist or didn't actually brew. There's one source that I've used that's especially suspect. It's the MAINE BUSINESS DIRECTORY, published now and again from the 1850s well into this century. It lists quite a number of people as "beer manufacturers" or "brewers" who

Since The Dawn Of Time...

Beer - defined by WEBSTER'S as "a mildly alcoholic drink made from malt, hops, etc." - has been around a long, long time. Over 4,000 years before the birth of Christ, the Babylonians enjoyed a beerlike beverage. Actually, beverage<u>s</u>: they brewed 15 types of beer, including pale beer, dark beer, red beer, beer with a head, and beer without a head. The Egyptians called their beer "hek" and made it by crumbling chunks of barley bread into jars of water and allowing the mixture to ferment. For those unpleasant trips across the desert, only the fermented bread crumbs were brought along. When an oasis was reached, water was added and, voilà, the result was instant beer. The Egyptians knew the health value of beer, too. Pharmacists of the day relied on 700 prescriptions, 100 of which contained beer. The Greeks, as well, liked their brew. Noted philosopher Herodotus wrote a treatise on beer in 460 B.C., while Sophocles had a diet he favored for moderation. Its mainstays were bread, meat, lots of vegetables, and, of course, beer.

America has always been big on beer, too. On his fourth voyage to the New World, in 1502, Columbus discovered that the natives of Central America enjoyed a beerlike beverage made from maize (corn). He likened it to English beer. America's first "help wanted" ad ran in a London newspaper in 1609. It was for brewers to come to Virginia. And, speaking of Virginia, it was there that the Pilgrims intended to take up residence. But they settled for New England, in 1620, because supplies aboard the Mayflower were running low... most importantly their beer. A diary kept by one of those on board explained: "We could not now take time for further search or consideration, our victuals being much spent, especially our beere."

The Pilgrims had to overcome many a hardship, not the least of which was a lack of barley. But perseverance won out, as evidenced by these lines penned by one of the stouthearted group:

If barley be wanting to make into malt,
We must be content and think it no fault,
For we can make liquor to sweeten our lips,
Of pumpkins, and parsnips, and walnut tree chips.

In 1613 Dutch explorer Adrian Block (for whom Block Island is named) erected several log houses at the southern tip of Manhattan Island, one of which was converted to a brewhouse... the first "brewery" in the New World. Nor did "New Worlders" take their brewing lightly. In 1640 the Massachusetts Bay Colony passed a regulation that "No one should be allowed to brew beer unless he is a good brewer," while New York, in 1655, ruled it illegal for anyone to brew beer for sale unless they possessed "sufficient skill and knowledge in the art and mystery of brewing."

Stone Street, in lower New York City, became the first paved street in America in 1657. Originally named Brouwer (Brewer) Street, its paving was necessitated by the breweries located on it: the breweries' delivery wagons, laden with beer, kept getting stuck in the mud.

Famous early Americans who respected beer include William

George Washington had a great fondness for beer, especially porter. In fact, a recipe for making beer, written out in his own handwriting, still exists from 1757.

Penn (who had a brewhouse erected at his estate, Pennsbury), General Israel Putnam (who was, in real life, a brewer and tavernkeeper from Brooklyn, Connecticut), Thomas Jefferson (who, in an 1816 letter to a friend, discussed beer and stated "I wish to see this beverage become common."), and James Madison (who expressed his hope that "the brewing industry would strike deep root in every state of the Union").

And, finally, America's first privately endowed college for women, Vassar, was founded by wealthy Poughkeepsie ale brewer Matthew Vassar in 1861. And to this day Vassar students pay him tribute by occasionally bursting into song:

And so you see, for old V.C.
Our love shall never fail.
Full well we know
That all we owe
To Matthew Vassar's ale!

Cheers!

do not show up in any other source. And, in at least two instances, people were listed as still doing some brewing long after they were dead. That's a pretty good trick. Nevertheless, there's no way to invalidate the DIRECTORY's listings, either. They are included.

But, for all the things we don't know for sure, there are a few things we do know for sure. We know, first of all, that our pioneer Maine breweries were small. Perhaps even minute. They were micros before there were micros. Secondly, we know that our early brewers were entitled, if anyone ever was, to say their brews were handcrafted. There was no fancy equipment in their five-year plans. And, lastly, we know that they were a gutsy group. To be a brewer in a strongly temperance state could not have been easy.

The Brewers: It's Quite A Team

The most logical way to present our old-time brewers seemed to be county-by-county. So that's the way we've done it.

Alphabetically, ANDROSCOGGIN comes first. It's a good choice. The county that gives us L/A gave us a whole host of old-time brewers. And spread across four cities and towns, too.

First comes Auburn and Robert Newton. Born in Buckenfield, Chester, England in 1849, Newton came to America as a youth. At first he worked as a laborer, then ventured into the beer business, circa 1884, brewing small beer as well as hop and spruce beer. His "brewery" was his home, first at 39 First Street (now Riverside Drive), then at 7 Third Street, both in New Auburn. At some point in the 1890s he retired from brewing, working as a watchman until his death at age 64 in Auburn in September 1913.

Auburn's second brewer was George E. Kilbourne. Born in Auburn in 1858, Kilbourne founded the Crystal Fountain Bottling Co. in the basement of his house at 118 Main Street/27 Miller Street circa 1890, manufacturing soda and "All Kinds Of Small Beer." Circa 1892 he changed the company name to The Kilbourne Bottling Works, but his address and his product line remained the same. By 1895 Kilbourne was out of brewing and his own business and was working for the Windsor Mineral Spring Co. on Hogan Road in Lewiston. He died, from complications following the grippe, at the young age of 47 in Auburn in May 1905.

Lewiston's first commercial brewer of record was one Albert W. Potter, who is listed as a "Pop and Beer Manufacturer" at his house on Main Street, near Lincoln, in the early 1870s... and who inspired, one way or the other, a modest tidal wave of followers. He first appears to have entered into a brief partnership with a man named Morrill, as Potter and Morrill, circa 1873. By 1874 Potter, himself, was out of the picture and Morrill had teamed up with a Fred Thornton - as "Morrill & Thornton, Beer and Soda Water Mnfrs." - on Lower Main Street. That partnership, too, was soon dissolved, and by 1875-76 Fred Thornton was on his own as a "Beer Maker" in his house at 6 Lower Main.

Actually, he wasn't fully on his own: he was joined there by a man named Henry Hines. Within two years, though, Thornton had foregone brewing to become a stone mason, and Henry Hines was the man in charge of making beer at 6 Lower Main Street. By 1879 Henry, too, had moved on. The succession ended. And so did the brewing.

Next, chronologically, came John French, a shoemaker-turned-bottler. Operating out of his house at 56 Blake Street, French bottled beer and mineral water circa 1873-75. There are indications that he brewed what he bottled, but there is no certainty of it, and nothing else is known about him.

Our next-to-last Lewiston brewer is Joshua P. Maddox. Maddox came to Lewiston via Portland, where he'd been a grocery store clerk, and a saloonkeeper at 27 India Street. In fact, he's thought to have done a little brewing along with the saloonkeeping. (It's called a brewpub today!). In any case, he arrived in Lewiston circa 1886 and brewed small beer there, at 197 Main Street, until 1888 or so. He then returned to Portland, becoming an employee at his family's Maddox Wire Belting Company.

Lewiston's last old-time brewer is Augustus R. Stanton, who may or may not have brewed the real thing. We know he started out, in partnership with a Charles Skinner, in 1890. They called themselves Stanton & Skinner, were located at 6 Ash Street, and definitely did not brew "real" beer. Their creation was called Standard Hop Beer, and was billed as "The Great Temperance Drink Appetizer." By 1893,

though, Stanton was on his own and listed as a "Beer Manufacturer" at 7 Canal Street. He continued with the same listing, although changing his address to 440 Sabattus, through 1899. (Actually, in that very last listing, for 1898-99, a printer's error has Stanton as a "Beef Manufacturer."). Nothing is known of him after 1899.

Two other Androscoggin communities contributed brewers. They were Mechanic Falls and Wales. For at least a decade, from 1868 to 1878, F.A. Millett turned out small quantities of beer in Mechanic Falls. Wales' contribution was more short-lived: a man name Sylvanus Foss is believed to have done a small - probably *very* small - amount of commercial brewing in the 1868-1870 period.

I could find but one surviving structure from these various and diverse "breweries" that once adorned Androscoggin County. Parking lots and newer buildings have taken their toll. And the one survivor is just hanging in there. It's George E. Kilbourne's old operation at 118 Main Street, corner of Miller Street (just around the corner from today's Great Falls Brewing Company). It was most recently occupied by Leonard's Quality Carpets. Today it's boarded up and occupied by no one. I asked Denis Lemieux of Auburn, the structure's present-day owner, about its future. He was not encouraging. In fact he told me flat out that the building, which he believes goes back to at least the 1870s, is "completely deteriorated and structurally unsound" and that it is not included in any future plan he has for the site. In

"...it is as perfect a beverage
ale as any the market offers."

Ad, Portland *Daily Eastern Argus*, July 1, 1861.

other words, the building will be demolished.

In AROOSTOOK COUNTY we have - or don't have - J. Dunn. Dunn is the first of quite a few "brewers" who appear in the pages of the MAINE BUSINESS DIRECTORY, but appear nowhere else. The DIRECTORY lists Dunn under brewers in its 1867-68 edition. In Maysville, no less. However, Anna McGrath, Special Collections' Librarian at the University of Maine at Presque Isle, could find nothing on him/her in her reference materials. So we really don't know. We do know that Maysville itself ceased to exist as a town in 1883. It was annexed by Presque Isle that year.

Maine's most populous county, CUMBERLAND, saw brewers in both Cape Elizabeth/South Portland and Portland.

Cape Elizabeth comes first, and its brewery was a good one. It was the Forest City Brewery. And it was big. The brewery was founded in November 1858 by John Bradley and the McGlinchy brothers, James and Patrick. After but 16 months, however, the McGlinchys went their own way (see pages 24–25 and 27–28), with John Bradley taking over as sole proprietor. That was February of 1860.

John Bradley knew what he was doing. He'd already gotten his feet wet with respect to commercial brewing by doing a small amount of it in his home at 17 York Street, Portland, in the years around 1863-64. In Cape Elizabeth, he merely continued... but on a much grander scale. A professional brewmaster was brought in from the highly respected Taylor & Sons'

Portland brewery ads, 1859-1874. All except one are from the *Daily Eastern Argus*, Portland's reigning newspaper (and a staunch opponent of Neal Dow!) of the day. The one exception is the P. McGlinchy ad. It is from the MAINE BUSINESS DIRECTORY for 1869.

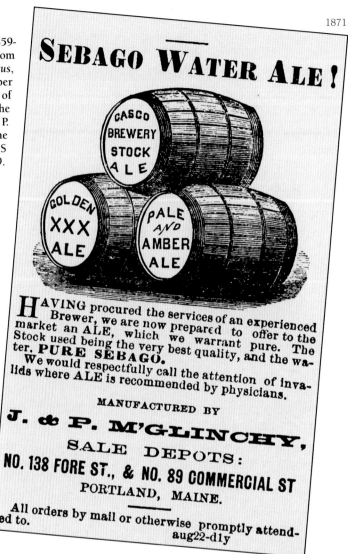

1871

Brewery of Albany, New York. The result was a series of 1859 ads that proclaimed, and probably justly so, that the ale manufactured at the Forest City Brewery was "as good as can be purchased at any other Brewery in the country." In late February 1860, John Bradley, now on his own, went a step further: he included a doctor's sworn statement that tests he'd conducted "established the entire purity of the materials used, and the high quality of the ale produced." But the doctor wasn't through. He continued: "The abundance of malt used in manufacturing this ale gives it the essential qualities found in the best kinds, either foreign or domestic; and being free from acid, it is as perfect a beverage ale as any the market offers." It was, in other words, just what the doctor ordered!

John Bradley manufactured a full line of ales - pale, amber, cream, and porter - in Cape Elizabeth until circa 1872. He then reverted

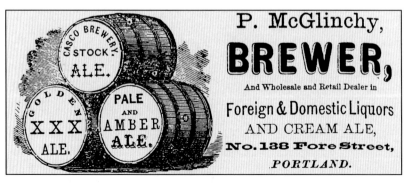

1869

back to a much smaller brewing effort at 17 York Street in Portland. Circa 1875 he retired from that, too. In 1881-82 he operated a saloon, still at 17 York Street, for a time. From then on, however, he appears to have been fully retired. He died in Cape Elizabeth in March of 1888, aged 73.

The Forest City Brewery, as large as it seemingly was, vanished without a trace. In his excellent 1965 book, A HISTORY OF CAPE ELIZABETH, MAINE, William B. Jordan, Jr. wrote that the former brewery was used as a canning factory in the early 1880s, and then burned to the ground in September of 1883. On its former site, where Highland Avenue crosses Ocean Street in South Portland (part of Cape Elizabeth was spun off to form South Portland in 1895), is now the side yard of the small structure that houses Clarence B. Kneeland's Bookkeeping Service. Back in Portland, 17 York Street didn't fare much better: on the site (since renumbered to 51-53 York) there is now a 1920 building that houses the Sports Action Sports Bar.

One final note re the Forest City Brewery. In his book, William B. Jordan, Jr. wrote that the spent grain from the brewery "was sold locally as cattle feed and was considered by many to greatly enhance the flavor of the milk." In a conversation I had with Mr. Jordan in mid-1995 he chuckled and added a postscript that I like a lot. "It (the spent grain) probably put a better head on the milk," he said.

Also in Cape Elizabeth is James Healy. Healy appears to have done a very small amount of commercial brewing, probably in his house, circa 1869. Nothing is known of him before or after.

It's Portland time. And "The Metropolis of Maine" does not disappoint. As is the case today, the Forest City was a veritable brewing mecca - by northern New England standards - in days of yore.

Brewer number one, alphabetically, is John Harrison. Harrison was a longtime Portland grocer who decided to branch into brew in 1870. When he did he borrowed a page out of John Bradley's book: he, too, named his endeavor the Forest City Brewery. Joining him as "beerbrewers" - the term of the day - were former sausage maker Robert B. Henry and former merchant James McLaughlin. Within a year or so, by the fall of 1871, they'd done more than join Harrison... they'd bought him out. Pale and amber ales as well as porter were their brews. And the brewery was still named Forest City. Within another year, however, it was all history. Forest City Brewery number two went the way of number one. It went out of business.

After their brewing adventures, James McLaughlin became first a dealer in flour and corn and then proprietor of a lunchroom on Federal Street. Robert Henry left Portland. John Harrison returned fulltime to the grocery business. But their venture had, at the very least, served to inspire another Harrison to try his hand at beer. That was John's brother, James, who operated a brewhouse at 53 Commercial Street during the years 1874 to 1876. James later moved to Lynn, Massachusetts where he passed away at age 74 in 1894. James McLaughlin died in Portland in May 1878. What became of John Harrison and Robert B. Henry is unknown.

The Forest City Brewery, rather substantial for its time, was located at 206 Fore Street. But renumbering* has played tricks: whereas today 206 Fore Street is across from Jordan's Meats, the original 206 Fore was halfway up Munjoy Hill between two no-longer-in-existence streets, School House Lane and Freeman's Lane. On the left side of Fore heading up the Hill between Mountfort and Waterville streets, the former brewery's site is today included within the Munjoy South Townhouse complex (just, it's nice to be able to say, a good barrel roll from the present-day Shipyard Brewery). James Harrison's former brewing site, 53 Commercial Street, no longer exists, either. It is now part of the Franklin Arterial's intersection with Commercial.

James Herbert is a puzzle. In both the 1886 and the 1889 editions of the MAINE BUSINESS DIRECTORY he is listed as a brewer of small beer at 221 Federal Street. But at no time is he ever so listed in the PORTLAND CITY DIREC- TORY. There he's listed as a waiter at the Preble House in the 1884 edition and then the opera- tor of a boarding house - at 221 Federal - in the 1886 through 1890 editions. It's possible that

Cont'd. on page 20

* In the 1870s many of Portland's streets were renumbered. As a result, what was #10 Doe Street in 1870 might be #82 Doe Street today.

"...and all kinds of Beers." Trade card, circa 1895. William Smallwood was a Patten har- ness maker and jack of all trades from 1890 to 1909. The "Beers" that he sold may or may not have been the real article.

ELLSLER.

WM. SMALLWOOD,
MANUFACTURER OF HARNESSES,
Also, all kinds of Repairing done neatly and cheap.
☞P. S. We keep Fruit and Confectionery, Cake and Pies, Tobacco, Cigars, and all kinds of Beers.
Patten, - - - Maine.

The Maine Law

"No person shall be allowed at any time,

to manufacture or sell, by himself, his

clerk, servant or agent, directly or

indirectly, any spirituous or intoxicating

liquors, or any mixed liquors, a part of

which is spirituous or intoxicating, except

as hereafter provided."

So begins what was officially known as *"An Act for the Suppression of Drinking Houses and Tippling Shops,"* but became much better known as the "Maine Law." Signed into effect by Governor John Hubbard in May 1851, it remained in force, except for a two-year period from 1856 to 1858, until superceded by National Prohibition in 1920.

The Maine Law was noble in intent. The almost lifelong vision of Maine native Neal Dow - two-time Mayor of Portland, Civil War general, and the man they called "The Napoleon of Prohibition" - it made Maine the first state to outlaw alcohol. It was noble. But it was doomed to failure.

The Maine Law prohibited the sale or manufacture of spirituous beverages... but it did not prohibit the drinking of them (except to the point of intoxication). Nor did it effectively prohibit their sale or manufacture, either. Alcoholic beverages were allowed to be manufactured and sold for "medicinal or mechanical purposes." Each town and city was instructed to set up its own agent, and he/she was permitted "to sell at some central or convenient place within said town or city, spirits, wines, or other intoxicating liquors"... as long as the medical or mechanical stipulation was met. And a lot of medical or mechanical stipulations were met!

People of affluence, however, didn't even have to go through the medicinal/mechanical subterfuge. They'd merely have what they wanted shipped in - by the case - from out of state. The liquor merchants of Boston, especially, did a land-office business in Maine. I recently acquired a PISCATAQUIS COUNTY BUSINESS AND RESIDENTIAL DIRECTORY for the year 1907. In it there are not five, not ten, but 14 Boston booze ads. All you had to do was fill out an order and enclose payment and your Jungle Rye ("Four Full Quarts = $2.85") or Old Mackinaw Rye ("12 Quarts = $12.00") or whatever would be shipped express-prepaid. And remember, this was Piscataquis County - Dover and Foxcroft and Milo and Brownville Junction - not the "evil" big cities of Portland, Lewiston, or Bangor.

But one didn't really even have to send to Boston for one's booze. The newspapers of the day make it quite evident that alcohol, in one form or another, was not too terribly difficult to come by in almost any community in the state. There were all kinds of tricks of the liquor trade. The Maine Law forbade selling spirituous beverages... but said nothing about giving them away. And, according to John Kobler in his 1973 book, ARDENT SPIRITS: THE RISE AND FALL OF PROHIBITION, that's just what a number of Portland grogshop proprietors did: sell a pickle or a slab of cheese at an exorbitant price... and give rum or ale away. In Bangor there was what was politely known as the "Bangor Plan," under which saloon and hotel owners would appear in court twice a year, plead guilty to the sale of alcohol, pay a fine... and then be allowed to go back and sell alcohol for the next six months. (In fact, everyone's favorite axe-wielder, Carrie Nation, heard of these goings-on and paid a visit to Bangor, specifically the well-known Bangor House. Although she found nothing – Bangor House management had been tipped off and had hidden the goods – Ms. Nation would later write in her memoirs that the Bangor House was "the worst rumseller in the whole country.").

In Portland there were so many liquor violation cases that, per a Portland *Evening Express* article of July 1901, lawyers were jockeying for position in the corridors of City Hall in order to get their best shot at potential clients.

Drinking - in a state that was supposed to be dry - was so rampant that many people found relief in laughing at it all. Newspaper article headlines, about raids and such, were often comical. My favorite, about a poor fellow who over-imbibed and was then robbed, is "Awoke From Booze Snooze With Head Funny And No Money" (Portland *Daily Eastern Argus*, July 1, 1915). Then there's the story about one of Maine's most esteemed sons, long-time Congressman Thomas B. Reed. While at a dinner in New York City in late 1899, Reed was chided about the Maine Law. Reed responded, with a straight face, that the Law had caused Maine men to lose all taste for liquor. That was met with howls of laughter and derision. Reed, still not cracking so much

as a smile, retorted that the popular belief that Maine prohibition wasn't working was due to the fact that whenever a New Yorker went to Maine the hospitable people of the Pine Tree State broke the law and served him a drink in order to save his life.

Things became so farcical that, in June of 1915, the Reverend Wilbur F. Berry of Augusta strongly suggested to Governor Oakley C. Curtis that he call out the state militia to put an end to the blatant violations of Maine's prohibition statutes. The governor responded that he did not have the power that would be necessary to enforce the statutes. In fact, further responded the governor, "It might be wise for Rev. Berry to go into politics and be a candidate for office, and thereby enforce the law himself." It was as apt a summation of the futility of the Maine Law as you're likely to find.

The price was right. Ad, PISCATAQUIS COUNTY BUSINESS AND RESIDENTIAL DIRECTORY, 1907.

he brewed a little and maintained the boarding house a little. Make beds in the morning; make beer in the afternoon. Why not? Whatever, it all came to an end in December 1892. That's when James Herbert died.

From bricks to beer: that's the story of James Hindle (sometimes spelled "Hindall"). Call it a mid-life crisis or call it just a taste for something new... but as he approached the age of 40 James Hindle changed his occupation from brickmaker to brewer. The year was circa 1842. His brewery was as homemade as his beer: it was right there in his house at 3 Neal Street... hardly something to bestir the big boys in Milwaukee or St. Louis or Cincinnati or Brooklyn. Yet it's an operation that must have been successful: between James (who died in December of 1867) and his son Charles (who died in April of 1888), it would remain in business a rather impressive 40 years or so. Charles, who shows up as part of Portland's brewing community circa 1861, moved operations to 115 Brackett Street around the time the Civil War ended, in 1865. There he would remain until he moved the business back to the family's home at 3 Neal in 1870 or so. He ceased brewing circa 1872. Today, what was 115 Brackett is 271 Brackett and the Hindle "brewery" is long gone, replaced by a multiple-dwelling apartment house built in 1910. The Hindle operation on Neal Street, due to renumbering, is even more complicated. The city completely reversed the numbers and changed sides of the street, too. As a result, if there were a number 3 Neal today - which there isn't - it would be down by Clifford or Spring Street. Instead, the original number 3 was right off Congress Street. It, too, is long gone. On the site now is 180 Neal (owned, ironically, by Richard Pfeffer of Gritty McDuff's renown!), built in 1910.

Next in Portland's veritable parade of yester-year brewers is the Ingalls brothers, Robert and Hiram. Natives of Shelburne, New Hampshire, both made the move to Portland in the 1860s. First came Robert, who set himself up as a small commercial brewer at 26 Portland Street in 1864. After service in the navy during the Civil War, Hiram made Portland his home, too. At first Hiram operated on his own, as a bottler at 82 Franklin Street. By 1868, though, the two had joined forces at 26 Portland. There they appear to have brewed and bottled a wide variety of both "hard" and "soft" beers as well as a full line of soda. Business was good and, in 1871 or 1872, the brothers moved to larger quarters at 13-17 Preble Street. They also changed their company name from R. & H.P. Ingalls to Ingalls Brothers. As the years went by the brothers decreased their interest in brewing and increased their interest in the manufacture and bottling of soft drinks. They still acted as a distributor of beer and ale; they just, after 1880 or so, didn't brew it themselves. Ginger ale, in fact, became their real speciality. And they were not at all bashful about proclaiming its merits: at one point they even went so far as to herald it as "The Best in the World."

In 1892 the brothers moved again, to even larger facilities at 36-40 Plum Street. A write-up on

Cont'd. on page 24

Artwork, *The Prism* (yearbook of the University of Maine, Orono), 1911. The State of Maine may have been "dry," but its towns and cities weren't. Its colleges probably weren't, either. Yearbooks of the period often make reference to beer and booze. Two examples I like are:

"Some of the first year men are wondering, if Carrie Nation should come to Bangor, as recently intimated by the local branch of the W.C.T.U., would law students find it more difficult to get admitted to the Bar."
(*The Prism*, 1902)

"Strong beer, a damsel smartly dressed, stinging tobacco, these I love best."
(*The Bowdoin Bugle*, 1904: wish list of James Philip Marston of Hallowell, Class of 1905)

Ad, BANGOR CITY
DIRECTORY, 1899

Advertising card,
circa 1900

Even in its brewing "heyday" in the 1870s, Maine's old-time beer production was never really very substantial. The peak year was most likely 1875, when 11,527 barrels were produced. That works out to 357,337 gallons. If it sounds impressive, it really wasn't: the nation's total for that year was 8,383,720 barrels (259,895,320 gallons!). As a result, brewers from Massachusetts, New York, New Hampshire and elsewhere "helped out." Shown here are ads, both from 1899, from two such "helpers."

NORFOLK BREWERY

BOSTON, MASS.

H. W. HABICH.   HABICH & CO.   EDWARD RUHL.

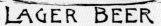

NORFOLK CABINET

LAGER BEER

FOR THE NEEDS OF PHYSICIANS, DRUGGISTS, ETC. AND FOR TABLE USE.

BOTTLED WITH ESPECIAL CARE AT OUR BOTTLING ESTABLISHMENT IN ROXBURY,

WE ARE TRYING TO GET AS NEAR AS POSSIBLE TO THE PHYSICIAN'S IDEA.

Combining these two:—

A MILD STIMULANT;

A WHOLESOME, NUTRITIOUS TONIC.

Such is our **NORFOLK CABINET LAGER**. It has been prepared with the special desire to supply to the medical profession a brewing of hops and malt which should have a lower per cent. of alcohol, making a milder stimulant for their patients than ordinary Lager beer, but maintaining the wholesome tonic action so much desired.

We have taken great pains to secure the finest and choicest barley malt for this special brand (**NORFOLK CABINET LAGER**) and use only the first quality of hops from the finest hop-growing districts, and by treating them in the proper manner we have succeeded in preserving in our Cabinet Lager the full, rich aroma of the hops so much desired by connoisseurs.

It is bottled in handsome white bottles, the stoppers of which are the *seals*, which are used once only and then discarded. This is the cleanest and most desirable way to close lager beer bottles.

We especially seek to introduce this brand of Lager Beer to families who are fastidious in their selection, and will appreciate a high-grade brewing which combines the important essentials named at the head of this circular.

A trial order is solicited.

General Agents for Bangor and vicinity.

McGUIRE BROS.,

154 Main Street,   BANGOR, MAINE.

Beer Powder Manufacturers.
AMERICAN BEER POW-
DER CO. Thompson &
Walsh (see adv. dept. p. 45).
Thomaston

The American Beer Powder Co.

You can imagine my excitement when I ran across the above listing in the MAINE BUSINESS DIRECTORY for 1867-68. Had Thomaston been on the threshold of instant beer? Was it on the cusp of revolutionizing the beer industry? (Hello, Thomaston; Bye bye, Milwaukee!).

Alas, however, a little research put a damper on the excitement. As Betty Robinson, president of the Thomaston Historical Society, explains it: George Thompson and Edwin Walsh, proprietors of American Beer Powder, were first and foremost proprietors of a local grocery/general store. A search of Thompson and Walsh's deed for 1867, in the collection of the historical society, lists an inventory of equipment, and it clearly shows there was no beer-making apparatus. Betty sums up the situation thusly: "The most likely thought is that, since it was a grocery store, the powder was for making root beer." I suspect Betty's right.

Ingalls Brothers in 1897 stated that their business had grown to "so great dimensions that from fifteen to twenty-five employees are needed to fill the orders."

Robert Ingalls passed away in January of 1900. Hiram kept on rolling, however, until he sold the operation in 1910. He passed away, at age 82, in 1921. The business he and his brother had founded continued on until 1934. Today, though, there are no remnants of its existence. Both 26 (since renumbered to 54) Portland Street and 13-17 Preble Street are now home to parking lots, while 36-40 Plum, as well as every other building that once adorned Plum, has long since been demolished. In fact, Plum Street - which used to be parallel to and midway between Exchange and Union streets, running from Fore to Middle - is itself now completely gone.

Following the Ingalls brothers are the McGlinchy brothers, James and Patrick, and if you partook of a brew anywhere in the world between Casco Bay and Back Cove in the 1860s or 1870s the chances are the brew you partook of was theirs. The McGlinchys were big. So big, in beer as well as many other businesses, that James H. Mundy in his 1990 book, HARD TIMES, HARD MEN: MAINE AND THE IRISH, likened them to another set of brothers. "The McGlinchys," wrote Mundy, " bring to mind a later family of brothers, the Earps of Dodge City and Tombstone. Both," continued Mundy, "were neither good nor bad, just tough, street-wise and shrewd."

Born in Ireland - Patrick in 1817 and James in

1823 - the brothers were to make their mark in Portland. Both became real estate barons and, by 19th century Maine standards, beer barons, too. Their first brewing venture appears to be when they joined forces with John Bradley, in November 1858, in the operation of a fledgling brewery on Ocean House Road in Cape Elizabeth (now South Portland: see page 13). Named the Forest City Brewery/McGlinchy, Bradley, & Co., it was a venture that lasted but 16 months, until February of 1860. Then "Handsome Jimmy" and Patrick were off on

I Found My Fill On Munjoy Hill

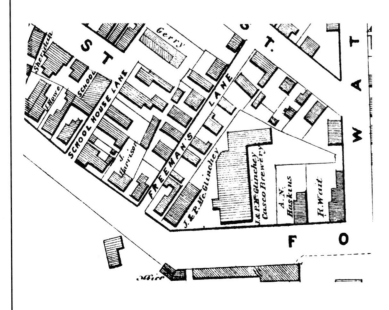

A look back at eastern Munjoy Hill, via the ATLAS OF CUMBERLAND CO., MAINE (published by the delightfully-named F.W. Beers & Co., of New York City, in 1871), clearly shows the scope of James and Patrick McGlinchy's Casco Brewery. John Harrison's operation can be seen as well. The street on the right is Waterville Street. That's Fore at the bottom. Freeman's Lane and School House Lane no longer exist. Much of the area shown is today occupied by the Munjoy South Townhouses.

Ad, 1896

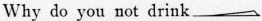

Why do you not drink

INGLESIDE GINGER ALE?

You will always find it at all First-Class Grocers. If not, send to the
. . . Manufacturers for a Trial Order. . . .

INGALLS BROTHERS,

36, 38 AND 40 PLUM STREET,

PORTLAND, - - - - MAINE.

Beginning as brewers in Portland in 1864, the Ingalls brothers, Robert and Hiram, eventually found the manufacture of soda and temperance drinks (beer-like beverages with little or no alcohol) to be more to their liking. The items pictured here are all from their non-beer years.

COMPLIMENTS OF
INGALLS BROTHERS,
—MANUFACTURERS OF—
THE FINEST
TEMPERANCE DRINKS
IN NEW ENGLAND.
Portland, Me.

(The above is imprinted on the back of both of the girl-with-the-bird trade cards).

Trade cards, circa 1895
Courtesy of Rick Poore, Standish

Advertising poster, circa 1900

their own. The result was the giant - for its day - Casco Brewery they constructed halfway up Munjoy Hill. Only ale was brewed. Their early newspaper ads, headlined ALE! ALE, ALE!! ALE, ALE, ALE!!, certainly made that perfectly clear! Later ads heralded the brothers' Casco Brewery stock ale, golden ale, and pale and amber ale. All, patrons were assured, were made with pure Sebago Lake water. Depots were maintained at 89 Commercial Street and 138-140 Fore Street, as well as at the brewery.

The McGlinchys were wildly successful... not only in the beer business but in the saloon, wholesale liquor, retail, and landlord trades as well. Even a glance at an 1870s' Portland ward map makes clear the tremendous number of properties marked "McGlinchy." By 1872, though, the brothers decided to go their separate ways with respect to the brewery. Their partnership was dissolved, "by mutual agreement," as of September 4, 1872. What happened after that is unclear. Both continued to be listed as brewers in the various city directories - James at 89 Commercial and Patrick at 138-140 Fore - but the odds are that these addresses were still depots and that the actual brewing took place, as before, on "the Hill." Two other members of the McGlinchy clan, William and Joseph, also made brief forays into brewing in the 1870s, William circa 1875 and Joseph circa 1877-1879.

James died, at age 57, in June of 1880. The *Portland Sunday Times* called him "industrious" and "generous"; "a credit as a man and citizen." James H. Mundy, writing 110 years later, labeled him "Portland's richest Irishman." "Wyatt Earp," he added, "would have been envious."

Patrick remained in the brewing business until 1882, then focused on his saloon holdings. He passed away, at age 71, in April 1888. Today the brothers' brewery on Munjoy Hill is completely gone. On its site, 51 Fore Street just below Waterville Street, (and just above where the McGlaughlin & Henry Forest City Brewery stood) there is now the Munjoy South Townhouse complex. Eighty-nine (since renumbered to 121-123) Commercial Street is now home to a pair of newer buildings, occupied by Angie's Pizza, and the Sail Loft Tavern. One-hundred thirty-eight to 144 (since renumbered to 342-344) Fore is now home to a parking lot.

Next-to-last is a George Smith, who did a small amount of brewing at his home at 25 Fore Street from circa 1865 to circa 1872. Other than that, nothing else is known about him.

Last in line came the Walkers, who could rightly be called Maine's first family of brewing. At least four of them - all seemingly related - were involved in the business of beer in Portland. Or wanted to be. Walker number one, John, appears to have never really gotten off the ground. But he had big plans. Circa 1851 he constructed a brewery in the basement of his Depot Hotel. Probably would have called it the Depot Hotel & Brewpub. Or maybe Gritty Walker's. We'll never know because the hotel folded in late 1851. Ads taken to try to rent the hotel - located adjacent to the old Portland, Saco & Portsmouth Railroad terminal, where State and Commercial streets intersected back when they still intersected - concluded, in fact, with a pitch for the brewery: "Also, to let, a Brewery under the Hotel. There are two large rooms, large boilers set in brick, a never failing supply of pure water by an aquaduct; the whole well fitted up and in perfect order for a Brewery."

The Depot Hotel brewery never made it. But John's dream does appear to have served as a catalyst. Within a year, Tristram Walker, who had been a porter at the hotel, began brewing commercially at his house at 46 Portland Street. That would have been around 1852. By 1856 Tristram had disappeared but the brewing continued on, still at 46 Portland Street. Benjamin F. Walker was the new brewer's name, and he would brew small beer - a low alcohol beer meant to be consumed shortly after brewing - for the next dozen years, changing locations as his business grew. Circa 1857 he moved operations a block away to 25 Alder Street. Around 1865 he moved the brewery again, this time to 303 Congress Street. And by 1868 he was on the move once more, to 366 Congress Street, where he was assisted by (his son?) Emery Walker.

Later described by the local press as "an industrious man," Benjamin F. Walker made a mistake circa 1869. He was a success in the beer business - and was "in comfortable circumstances," as one newspaper later reflected - but he decided to get out of beer and into fruit and confectionary. He shut down the brewing operation and opened a fruit and candy store at 355 Congress Street. It was a flop. Before too many moons had passed Benjamin was out of "comfortable circumstances" and deeply in debt. So deeply in debt he was sent to jail. Despondent, he committed suicide shortly after his release from jail. He died in Portland on February 19, 1876. Depending on which of the newspaper accounts you care to believe, he was "about 56," "about 58," or "about 65."

None of the Walkers' brewery buildings survive. Because of renumbering, the old numbers are not what they used to be. The Walkers' address at 46 Portland Street was in the block between Mechanic Street and Green Street (now Forest Avenue). It has long since been torn down. On its site today is Bintliff's Cafe and, to a lesser extent, Steve's Shoe Repair. Whereas today's 25 Alder Street would be on the corner of Oxford Street, the old 25 Alder was in the middle of the block, right about where the Salvation Army Thrift Store is today. What was 303 Congress Street is today 511 Congress, and on that site now is a D'Angelo Sandwich Shop. And, last of all, what was 366 Congress Street would have been part of the large site now occupied by the Baxter Building, 562 Congress, constructed in 1895.

FRANKLIN COUNTY's sole old-time brewer entry is Orrin Walker of the township of Freeman (near Strong). Born in Freeman in 1849, Orrin was primarily a farmer, but he's listed as a brewer in the MAINE BUSINESS DIRECTORY for both 1867-68 and 1869. He married four times, and died in Farmington in 1934. That's about all that's definitive that's known about him, but with the help of local historian George Thompson (who, with his wife F. Janet Thompson, is the author of the forthcoming book, FREEMAN, MAINE - A GENEALOGY) we are able to at least project somewhat with respect to Orrin. George reports that a large number of the people in Freeman grew hops at that time (the late 1860s); that the Walker family was a large family; that it would not be unlikely that they grew hops; and that it was quite possible that Orrin went one step further and converted the hops into beer. In fact, George ammended, it's "very, very likely."

I could find no old-time commercial brewers in **HANCOCK COUNTY.**

KENNEBEC COUNTY, thanks mostly to Waterville, scores very well on our old-time brewer rating scale. Alphabetically, though, Augusta leads off. The Capital City's contribution was Harmon W. Paine. Paine was co-owner of a fruit and confectionary store on Water Street, corner of Winthrop, until circa 1870 when he went on his own, setting up on Water Street opposite Granite Hall. He is believed to have brewed small beer as well as "pop beer" (most likely spruce and/or hop beer). By 1872 Paine had moved again, to Sewall Street, near Western Avenue. Here he continued to brew. The question is for how

These three ads are from the *Souvenir Programme, Second Annual Benefit, Portland Lodge, Benevolent and Protective Order of Elks*, held at the Portland Theatre on February 17th and 18th, 1893. As with the ads on 22 and 23, it was a case of out-of-state brewers being only too glad to "help out" and supply Maine with brew. The Alley Brewery, in Roxbury, Boston, was a sizable ale-only brewery that operated from 1886 to 1918, while Bergner & Engel brewed copious amounts of lager in far-off Philadelphia from 1869 to 1920. Van Nostrand's Bunker Hill Breweries, however, is the most noteworthy. From their twin breweries (one for ale; one for lager) in Charlestown, Massachusetts they supplied many a bottle and many a keg of their famous P.B. Ale. Other brands included Bunker Hill Lager, Boston Club Lager, and Old Musty Ale. With roots that stretched back to 1821, Van Nostrand operated until 1918.

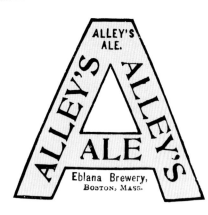

long. The MAINE BUSINESS DIRECTORY shows him operating at least through 1887. The Augusta/Gardiner/Hallowell city directories list him through 1877 or so. I'd go with the Augusta/Gardiner/Hallowell directories.

Next comes Hallowell and an operation that was begun by a man who was quite a guy. He was Joseph E. Howe, Sr., and he was born in Temple, Maine in 1807 and moved to Hallowell in 1828. He, too, at first established himself as a confectioner and, according to *The Hallowell Register*, he also "established a reputation for honest dealings and honest wares."

Left, a glorious lithographed poster from 1895, and, below, an advertising placard from circa 1895. "P.B." supposedly stood for "Purest and Best.

What really made Joseph E. Howe, Sr. so special, though, was his patriotic zeal. When the War Between The States broke out he followed three of his sons into the service of his country, signing on for two years. He was 54 at the time. And when those two years were up, he signed on for three more, serving until the end of the war. One does not have to be an M.I.T. graduate to figure out how old Joseph E. Howe, Sr. was when he was finally mustered out of the G.A.R. (He was 58!).

Returning to civilian life, J.E.H., Sr. jumped back into the world of candy and confectionary... until circa 1870, when he branched out, adding small beer and pop (lemon, spruce, and hop) beer to his line of "honest wares." Joining him were two of his sons, Frank and Joseph E., Jr. In fact, the endeavor was named J.E. Howe & Sons. Their address was Water Street, opposite Perley's Lane.

By the early 1880s, Joseph E. Howe, Sr. was feeling his age. He retired from both the candy and the beer business. (He died in January 1891, at age 83. In its obituary, *The Hallowell Register* honored him by calling him "one of our best citizens".). Taking over at the brewing end of things was a third son, Eugene L. Howe. In partnership with a former boardinghouse operator by the name of John Young he kept things going, as Young & Howe, "Bottlers and Beer Manufacturers," until circa 1897.

J.E. Howe & Sons' former address on Water Street, opposite Perley's Lane, is today a driveway. Young & Howe's location at 206 Water Street is an empty lot.

To Waterville, however, goes the honor of being the king of the county when it came to Kennebec's brewers. At least seven individuals tried their hand at brewing. Not much, however, is known about any of them. First in line was L.R. Marsh, who brewed small beer very briefly in the mid/late 1870s. Then there was Robert W. Armour. He set himself up on Common Street, across from City Hall, and brewed both hop and small beer as well as selling candy, fruit, and cigars and tobacco. He operated from circa 1875 to 1880 or so and then gave it all up to become a shoemaker. Next came the Wheelers - Sumner A. Wheeler, Sr. (1800-1887) and Sumner A. Wheeler, Jr (1834-1919) - who brewed small beer on Silver Street from circa 1875 to circa 1883. An F.C. Brackett ran a combination beer/soda/syrup/mineral water manufactory on Temple Street from 1876 to circa 1880. Further hedging his bets, he wholesaled candy and cigars as well. Next came J. Parlin Wyman, who's listed as a "Beer Mnfr." (first on Front Street and later at 3 Mechanic Square) from 1879 to 1886, and then as a "Soda Water Mnfr." at 3 Mechanic Square from 1887 to circa 1890. Last in Waterville's rather amazing line-up of old-time brewers is Charles T. Gardner (1834-1897; often spelled "Gardiner"), who manufactured small beer at 4 Main Street from circa 1879 to about 1883 before becoming a fruit/confectionary/cigar dealer at the same address.

With so few specific addresses it's difficult to tell if any of the Elm City's brewing abodes yet survive. But it's safe to say that the two for

Two postcard views of Portland's "Rum Room," where authorities stored the various and often diverse rum, whiskey, beer, alcohol-making apparatus, etc. that they confiscated during their various and often diverse raids...before

they, once a month, drained it all down the city's sewer system. The bottom view is circa 1908, when the Rum Room was located within City Hall. The top view is circa 1915, by which time the infamous Room had been transferred to the Cumberland County Courthouse. The men appearing triumphantly amidst the goods are identified as Deputy Sheriffs.

which there is a specific address do not. J. Parlin Wyman's structure at 3 Mechanic Square is long gone. In fact, just try asking around Waterville re Mechanic Square (which used to run north from 41 Temple Street): all you're likely to get is a blank stare. And 4 Main (where Charles T. Gardner used to hang his brewer's hat) is also history: the address is now included in the roadway just below the boarded-up-but-still-standing former Waterville Hardware store.

Camden and Rockland both chipped in with old-time **KNOX COUNTY** brewing efforts. Camden's contribution was Warren C. Mansfield, a man of many trades. During his 74 years (1833-1907), Mansfield was at one time or another a shoemaker, a seaman, an engineer, and a cook. And a brewer. Over the ten-year period between 1877 and 1887 he appears to have done a small amount of commercial brewing at his home on Mechanic Street.

Rockland's brewer of record was a gentleman with the rather distinctive name of Asahel U. Penniman. Penniman was primarily a proprietor of a fruit and confectionary store... but he is believed to have also brewed small beer in his home on Sea Street in the years from 1876 to 1880 or so.

In **LINCOLN COUNTY** the MAINE BUSINESS DIRECTORY for the year 1878 lists a John Mancey as a brewer of small beer in Wiscasset. But if a John Mancey did some brewing in "Maine's Prettiest Village" he sure didn't do it for long. Or with much fanfare. A quite thorough reading of Wiscasset Town Reports, death

records, cemetery records, and the four (believe it or not) weekly newspapers of the day* unearthed absolutely zip as far as John Mancey goes. So John was a short-timer at best. Brew and run. If he brewed at all.

In **OXFORD COUNTY**, Buckfield, Canton, and Rumford Point all saw a flurry of brewing activity, although there is little real record of any of it. Local history buff Virginia Smith could tell me nary a thing about the N.F. Shaw who is reputed to have done some commercial brewing in Buckfield in and around 1878. "I looked everywhere and couldn't find a thing," she reported. Virginia did add, however, that the good farmers in the area used to grow hops back in those days - "back in the dark ages," as she laughingly phrases it - and we agreed that might have inspired Mr. Shaw, whoever he was, to put up some brew.

Canton's contribution was one Orrin Leach, listed as a brewer in both the 1867-68 and 1869 editions of the MAINE BUSINESS DIRECTORY. Again, though, he doesn't ring any bells with local folks in the know. Canton history expert Gwen Campbell did a lot of digging - even "picked everyone's brain" at the Canton Historical Society - and could come up with not so much as a shred of information about Orrin. As Gwen said with a chuckle: "There

---

*Including one with the wonderful name of *The Seaside Oracle* and another with the even-more-wonderful name of *The Lilliputian*.

were probably plenty of stills around here but no one knows anything about any brewers." She did add, though, that a lot of Canton's old records have been destroyed in one flood or another. "We've had so many floods," she says ruefully.

Closing out Oxford County is Rumford Point and J. & I.H. Martin, listed as brewers in both the 1867-68 and the 1869 editions of the MAINE BUSINESS DIRECTORY. I wish there were a lot to report on them, but there isn't. Even noted Rumford historian Stuart Martin is stumped. "I never heard of any beer manufacturer around here," he told me. He did, however, tell me that hops were a big crop in the Rumford area in the 1860s. Barley was, too. Put the two together and you have a good start on making beer. That's most likely what J. and I.H. Martin did, although Stuart Martin could find not a mention of their venture in his extensive Rumford reference library. As the man who wrote both NEW PENNACOOK FOLKS–*the* definitive history of Rumford–and the long-running Down Memory Lane column in the *Rumford Falls Times* summed up: "It's kind of a mystery, I guess."

In **PENOBSCOT COUNTY** you'd expect "The Big B" - Bangor - to have had its share of brewing pioneers. It had. But, surprisingly, tiny East Corinth and even more tiny Carroll both saw some brewing activity as well.

Let's start with Bangor and the Flaherty brothers. In 1890 Peter L. and Dennis E. Flaherty got together and set up a small brewhouse in Peter's American House hotel (slogan: "For A Single Day A Single Dollar") at 14 Haymarket Square, where they produced a variety of small beers as well as crab apple cider, ginger ale, and something named standard nervina. Within a year or so, though, the partnership broke up. Dennis left to go into the retail clothing business; Peter kept the brewing and bottling operation going, moving it to 35 Exchange Street and changing its name from Flaherty Brothers to the Bangor Soda Company. Within another year, however, all went kaput. The brewing and bottling stopped. Dennis Flaherty died in February 1894. What became of Peter is unknown.

Next, alphabetically, comes Daniel T. Gallagher. After working as a clerk for a number of years, Gallagher ventured into brewing, circa 1883. Small beer was his product. "Front (Street), near May (Street)" was his business address. He appears to have brewed until 1886 or 1887. He then disappeared and nothing more is known about him.

Much, however, is known about our next brewer. He's Aaron A. Robinson and he was born in Harmony, Maine in 1835, moved first to Hermon, and then, when he was 21, to Bangor. For a time he operated a hauling business in partnership with his brother. He was then a dry goods merchant. In 1867 Robinson made his move into the world of soda and beer manufacturing, setting up shop first on Franklin Street, then 65 Broad, and then finally, circa 1878, in his house at 12 Birch Street. In 1881 he branched out into the ice business, forming Citizens' Ice Company with his son, Fred. He

cont'd. on page 39

1872

EMERY O. WALKER,

MANUFACTURER AND BOTTLER OF

SMALL BEER, SODA, Etc.,

CORNER OF MAIN & WATER STS.,

SACO, ME.

ALL ORDERS PROMPTLY ATTENDED TO.

BANGOR SODA CO.,

P. L. FLAHERTY, Prop.

Manufacturer of the Celebrated

Crab Apple Cider, Ginger Ale, Standard Nervina,

AND SMALL BEERS OF ALL KINDS.

35 Exchange Street,   Bangor, Maine.

1892

Ads from around-the-state brewers of yore, 1871-1892. The ads for Benjamin F. Haley and J.E. Howe & Sons promote "soft" beers only, but both of these firms are believed to have brewed "hard" beer as well. The Haley ad is especially intriguing. Looking at it, one might think that Haley oversaw an immense operation. He didn't. The illustration used in the ad was a stock cut...used to embellish many another ad, too.

J. E. HOWE & SONS,

Wholesale and Retail Dealers in

Confectionery.

Also Manufacturers of

LEMON, SPRUCE & HOP BEER,

WATER ST., opp. Perley's Lane,

HALLOWELL, ME.

J. E. Howe.   J. E. Howe, Jr.   F. B. Howe.

ALL CANDIES Warranted PURE.

1871

Billhead, John Bradley's Forest City
Brewery, 1860. This - apart from
newspaper advertisements - is one
of only two pieces of 19th century
Maine breweriana (an item of beer
advertising or packaging) known to
exist. In the entire world. I came
across it in a used book store in
Portland in 1987. I did not realize
its significance then. I do now.

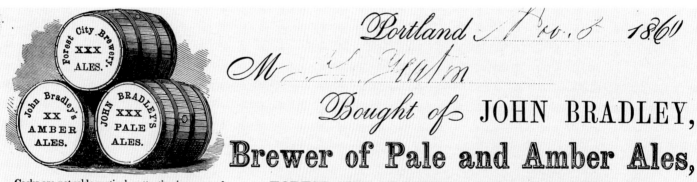

remained active in both businesses - although it appears he favored his ice venture at the expense of his beverage venture from the late 1880s on - until his death in December 1904. In its obituary, the *Bangor Daily News* wrote: "Mr. Robinson was always successful in his enterprises and was respected by all who knew him for his ability and integrity."

Our last old-time Bangor brewer, John A. Wallis, was truly a pioneer. His involvement with carbonated beverages goes back to 1842! Born in Guilford, Maine in 1818, he moved to Bangor with his family when he was ten, in 1828. His first paying job was as toll collector at the Orono Bridge, but in 1842 he decided it was to be the beverage business for him. He appears to have manufactured only soft drinks until 1872 or so... when he commenced to add small beer to his line-up.

Wallis had a number of early addresses but Kenduskeag Block was the one he called home the longest. Later addresses included 54 Exchange Street and 110 Exchange Street. According to an 1888 article on Wallis, he had a staff of "twelve experienced assistants" and "the use of a finely arranged and fitted-up building, four stories high." Sounds mighty impressive. The article, in the flowery style of the period, goes on to especially laud Wallis' soda selection and the fact that he was sole eastern Maine agent for "the celebrated Moxie Nerve Food." What the article had to say about Moxie - which was invented in Union, Maine in 1876 - is priceless: "This food is a harmless luxury; a luscious food beverage that prevents injury from luxurious living; that sustains the overstrained worker without harm; makes the nerves feel better and removes all the bad effects of stimulants and dissipation." Sounds even more impressive.

Moxie or not, John A. Wallis eventually died, in February of 1896. In its obituary, the *Daily Whig and Courier* newspaper wrote: "He was an able business man and in his social life was a genial friend to all who knew him, and he was held in the highest esteem by all for his sterling qualities."

As with Portland and Lewiston, Bangor's "breweries" of long ago do not appear to have fared well. All of lower Exchange Street, including numbers 35, 54, and 110, was torn down in the name of Urban Renewal in the 1960s. Where Aaron Robinson operated for a while, at 65 Broad, is now occupied by a vest-pocket park. Peter L. Flaherty's American House is long gone. Even the address "Haymarket Square" has ceased to exist. That leaves 12 Birch of those operations with a specific address. Due to renumbering, what was number 12 Birch during the days of Aaron Robinson would appear to now be 98 Birch. It's an older two-story/two-family structure and it may go back to the days of Robinson, but I don't think so. The City of Bangor's Tax Assessor Office lists the building as built "about 1900." My hunch is that it's more likely "about 1910"... and, therefore, too new to have experienced Robby's malt and/or soda pop creations.

Tiny Carroll (roughly midway between Lincoln and Topsfield) kicks in with one addition to Penobscot County's roll call. He's Josiah C. Collins and the MAINE BUSINESS DIRECTORY for 1869 lists him as a brewer. That's news, though, to local historian and author (of the 1995 book, THE CARROLL HILLS: THE WAY THINGS USED TO BE) Jane Thompson. She's never heard of Collins and could find no mention of him in the extensive research material at her disposal. But she ventures that there certainly could have been a brewer in Carroll. As she laughs, "The town was (legally) dry... but there were sure spirits available."

Rounding out Penobscot's brewing efforts of yesteryear is Charles Megquier of East Corinth. And, thanks to Corinth/East Corinth historian Pauline Sodermark, we know a considerable amount about him. According to Pauline (herself a distant niece of Megquier: he was her grandfather's uncle), Charles was born in Parkman, Maine in 1831, one of 14 children. His family moved to Corinth and there Charles involved himself in a whole host of occupations and responsibilities. He was primarily the proprietor of a combination dry goods store/pharmacy on Main Street in East Corinth, but he also ran a printing business and at one time or another served as Town Clerk, Justice of the Peace, and Deputy Sheriff. He is also listed as a brewer in the MAINE BUSINESS DIRECTORY for 1867-68, and for 1869. When I asked Pauline and her mother, Florence G. Young Sodermark (who's 91), if they thought Megquier did brew some real beer, Florence

upped and laughed and stated: "I'd accuse him of anything that would make money." And Pauline added that Charles Megquier was "a real entrepreneur." Pauline also felt that, although Corinth has historically been a "dry" town, the brewing of beer for "medicinal purposes" might have been acceptable for a pharmacist.

Charles Megquier died in 1908. His store (and brewhouse?) has long since burned down. On its site, at the intersection of Routes 15 and 43, there is today a United Bank office.

I could find no old-time commercial brewers in **PISCATAQUIS COUNTY**.

Did or did not Bath - and **SAGADAHOC COUNTY** - have a brewery? It's a good question. The 1876-1877 edition of GREENOUGH'S DIRECTORY FOR BATH, BRUNSWICK AND RICHMOND lists (Isaac C.) Gay & (E.H.) Elwell as a "beer manufacturer" on Front Street, corner of Oak. The directory previous to that, for the year 1874 (the directories were not published every year), lists neither gentleman. Nor does the following directory, for 1880. It appears mssrs. Gay and Elwell breezed into town and then breezed out. The 1876-1877 directory was published in 1876. The information included in it was most likely compiled in late 1875. However, a careful reading of the *Bath Daily Times* for the last half of 1875 failed to unearth even one Gay & Elwell ad or announcement. There were at least 200 ads for Dr. G. Ware Gay's Vegetable Restorative Pills ("a sure and speedy Remedy for Dyspepsia, Sick Headache, Dizziness,

This is a photo of Charles Megquier's operation, circa 1895. Charles' store was downstairs; Eli Parkman Post #119 G.A.R. was upstairs. Whatever the occasion for the photo was, it was obviously a grand one: there are people here and there and everywhere and they are sure all spiffed up.

Courtesy of Pauline Sodermark, Corinth.

Costiveness, Nervous Complaints, Disease of the Blood and Skin, and Female Complaints"), but not a single word from Gay & Elwell. So we don't know. Isaac and E.H. may have brewed a tonic or a spruce or a root beer (all soft drinks). Or they may have brewed the best darned lager that Sagadahoc County has ever been privileged to enjoy.

Secondly, the MAINE BUSINESS DIRECTORY for 1879 lists a W.F. Robinson as a brewer of small beer on Front Street, but neither Bath city directories nor newspaper ads and announcements of the day support it.

Did or did not Bath have a brewery? Take your pick.

Earning **SOMERSET COUNTY** a place in Maine brewing posterity is a man named James E. Frye. Again, though, it's a case of a listing in the MAINE BUSINESS DIRECTORY... and then nothing else. Frye, according to the DIRECTORY, did some brewing in Skowhegan from circa 1866 to circa 1870. But an extensive search by Judi Inchauteguiz, curator of the Skowhegan House of History, turned up not hide nor hair of Mr. Frye. As Judi was wont to point out, however, she wouldn't be at all surprised to find that Skowhegan did have a brewer back then. "After all," said she, "we had everything else here."

WALDO COUNTY's sole entry is Carlton & Company, in Winterport, listed as a brewer in the 1869 MAINE BUSINESS DIRECTORY. However, I could find no such firm listed in any other directory. Nor could local historian Don Weston find out a thing about Carlton &

Company, either. That may be because, by Don's rough estimate, "95% of the women living in Winterport at the time were probably W.C.T.U. members." When I commented that it was unlikely a brewer really did exist there under those circumstances, Don replied "Not necessarily... it'd just mean he had to be more secretive, that's all." Don then added: "It sounds like it might've been a good beer."

WASHINGTON COUNTY saw five possible pioneer brewers spread over two communities, Eastport and Machias. Eastport had three of them, although all three have been very largely forgotten over time and very little is known about them. The three show up as brewers only once, in the 1855 MAINE REGISTER. First comes Charles Andrew Jackson. Born in Fredericton, New Brunswick in December 1811, he appears to have been primarily a grocer and confectionary manufacturer who may or may not have also dabbled in beer briefly. He died in Eastport in 1888. Candidate number two is Edward Marshall about whom, alas, absolutely nothing is known. Candidate number three is John Kendall Norwood. And, other than that he was born in Eastport in November 1816, absolutely nothing is known about him, either. Is it possible that Eastport really had three "breweries" in the mid-1850s? It certainly is. After all, as local historian Frances Raye puts it so well, Eastport was "booming" in those days.

Machias had two pioneer brewers, albeit briefly. Both were men of many occupations. Number one was Warren P. Calligan, who did a small amount of commercial brewing in the mid-1850s on his way to becoming a printer (according to 1860 census records) and a painter (according to 1870 census records). Number two was Gilbert H. Longfellow, who also did a small amount of brewing in the mid-1850s on his way to becoming a butcher (1860 census records) and a merchant (1862 MAINE REGISTER). He'd earlier, according to the 1850 census, been a laborer. Local historian Val Atwood, from whom most of this information was received, also noted that Gilbert Longfellow's real estate holdings were valued at $3,000 in 1860, "a goodly amount for that time." Val suspects that Gilbert may have gone into the beer-making business in conjunction with his butcher business. She may well be right.

YORK COUNTY's largest community, Biddeford, can boast of having had four old-time brewers. That's a lot.

First, alphabetically, comes Leverett S. Baldwin, who set up operations at 38 Elm Street circa 1860, before moving to the rear of 60 Elm Street around 1868. There he brewed small beer until his death in 1870 or 1871.

Next is John Cantillon, who was probably more of a bottler than a brewer. He first shows up as a bottler of mineral water at 2 Pine Street in 1887-1888. By 1889 small beer was added to his roster, although it is unclear whether he brewed it or merely bottled it. He most likely did a little of both. Whatever, he remained in business, always at 2 Pine, until his demise in the early 1890s.

Biddeford brewer number three was far and away the longest-lasting and the most successful. He was Benjamin F. Haley, and he was born in Hollis, Maine in 1831, and then moved with his family to Limington when he was seven. In 1854 Haley took a Limington woman, Elmira Seavey, as his wife and then settled into what appeared to be a lifetime of Limington farming. But he was restless. He wanted more. And in 1859 he made the move to the bright lights of Biddeford.

At first he worked as a blacksmith. Then he worked as a carriagesmith (one who works on carriages). Then, circa 1871, he found his true calling: making beer and soda. In the beginning he set up at 29 Elm Street. Business boomed, however, and he soon found himself in need of larger quarters.

He moved to 8 Pine Street and there produced large - for the day - quantities of small beer as well as champagne cider, ginger ale, and root and spruce beer. "His spruce beer," it was written in an article in the *Biddeford Weekly Journal* in 1899, "was known the county over, as it was of his own concoction."

Benjamin F. Haley, in conjunction with his two sons, Alonzo and Charles, concocted and brewed and bottled for a rather remarkable 25-plus years, until 1897. He then sold the business and retired. He died in Biddeford in February of 1899.

Last comes a mystery man by the name of Benjamin M. Ridlon. Ridlon appears to have made small quantities of small beer at 61 Elm

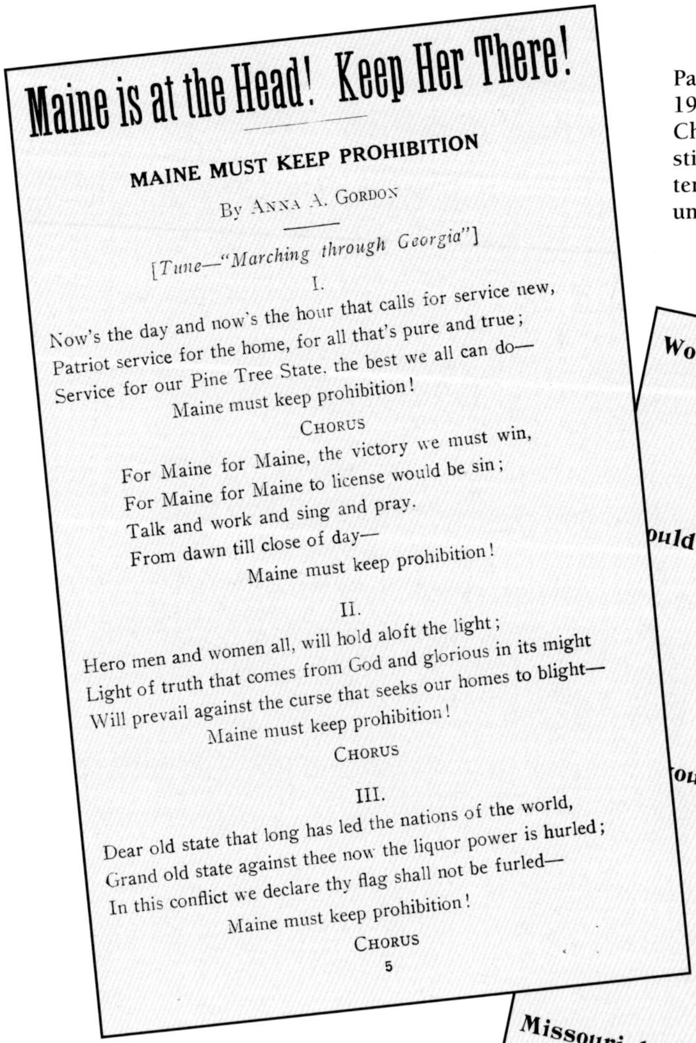

Maine is at the Head! Keep Her There!

MAINE MUST KEEP PROHIBITION

By Anna A. Gordon

[*Tune—"Marching through Georgia"*]

I.

Now's the day and now's the hour that calls for service new,
Patriot service for the home, for all that's pure and true;
Service for our Pine Tree State, the best we all can do—
Maine must keep prohibition!

CHORUS

For Maine for Maine, the victory we must win,
For Maine for Maine to license would be sin;
Talk and work and sing and pray,
From dawn till close of day—
Maine must keep prohibition!

II.

Hero men and women all, will hold aloft the light;
Light of truth that comes from God and glorious in its might
Will prevail against the curse that seeks our homes to blight—
Maine must keep prohibition!

CHORUS

III.

Dear old state that long has led the nations of the world,
Grand old state against thee now the liquor power is hurled;
In this conflict we declare thy flag shall not be furled—
Maine must keep prohibition!

CHORUS

5

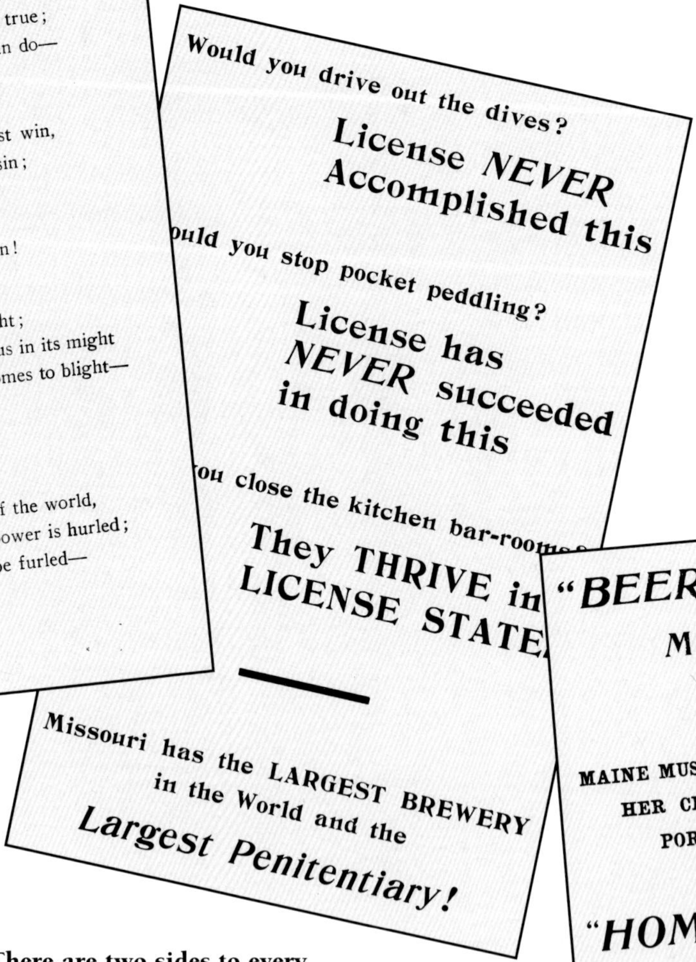

Pages from a W.C.T.U. pamphlet, 1911. The W.C.T.U. (Women's Christian Temperance Union) is still active in Maine, with headquarters in Portland and "auxillary unions throughout the state."

Would you drive out the dives?
License NEVER Accomplished this
ould you stop pocket peddling?
License has NEVER succeeded in doing this
ou close the kitchen bar-rooms
They THRIVE in LICENSE STATE
Missouri has the LARGEST BREWERY in the World and the
Largest Penitentiary!

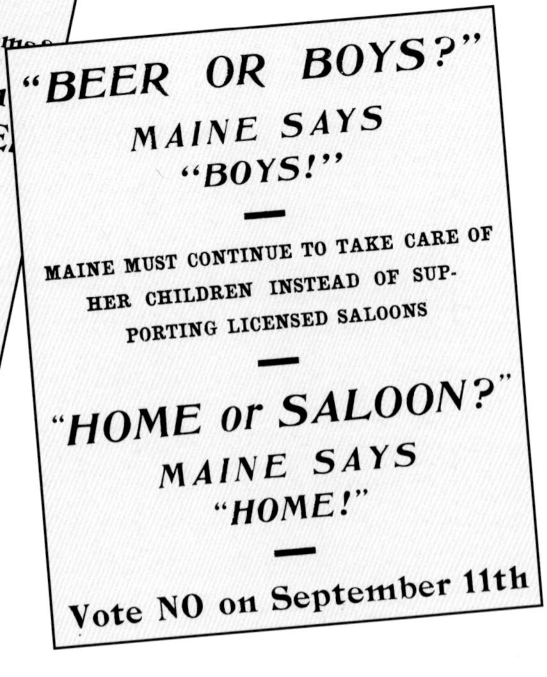

"BEER OR BOYS?" MAINE SAYS "BOYS!"

—

MAINE MUST CONTINUE TO TAKE CARE OF HER CHILDREN INSTEAD OF SUPPORTING LICENSED SALOONS

—

"HOME or SALOON?" MAINE SAYS "HOME!"

—

Vote NO on September 11th

Two Sides

There's an old saying that goes "There are two sides to every story." That is certainly the case here! On the one hand - on this page - is the "Beer Is Evil" posture put forth by Maine's many, many temperance organizations in days of yesteryear.

Ad, 1910. With origins that reached back to 1864, F.A. Poth & Sons operated until 1920, and then from 1933 to 1936.

Poth's Beer

IN THE STUDY

Men who work with their brains must find food for the brains—food that keeps the nerves steady and the head clear.

They drink beer. The world's greatest students—the German's—are the fathers of beer. They drink a good pure beer like Poth's—it's as fine a food as they can get.

Its mellowness—its richness in the best of hops—the nourishment of the malt—give it unequaled tonic properties. Clear, sparkling, enjoyable at all times to fogged brain or tired body.

If your bottler can't supply you, 'phone or write us.

F. A. POTH & SONS, Inc.

31st and Jefferson Sts., Phila., Pa.

Keystone Phone, Park, 874
Bell Phone, Poplar, 4511-12-13

On the other hand - on this page - is the "Beer Is Wonderful" posture put forth by many in the brewing industry.
Beer = Bad?
Beer = Good?
The truth is probably somewhere in between.

Is Beer A Vegetable?

A vicar advertised for a servant a short time ago, and a country girl, with a fat, red face, answered the advertisement.

After the vicar had asked a few personal questions he said:

"You know, we are all vegetarians here, and, of course, we should require you to be one. No meat, you know—simply vegetables."

She dropped her eyes and for a time seemed deep in thought. "Well, what do you think?" asked the vicar, after a short time. "Well, sir," she replied, "it's like this. I don't mind so much about the meat; but before I take the position I should like to know if you — er — call beer a vegetable?"

She was not engaged.

Joke, *Biddeford Daily Journal*,
August 23, 1913.

Street for several years in the early 1870s. Other than that, not a thing is known about him.

As is to be expected, none of Biddeford's brewing facilities of yore yet exist. Where numbers two and eight Pine Street once were is now parking space for Maine Glass, Inc. What was 29 Elm Street is also a parking lot, for Biddeford Tire and Auto Service. Where Leverett S. Baldwin did his brewing, at 60 Elm, there is now the circa 1930 Ralph Pill Electric Supply Company building. And mystery man Benjamin M. Ridlon's old locale at 61 Elm is now yet another parking lot.

North Berwick kicks in with one brewer old-timer. He was Howard S. Fall. Fall was primarily the proprietor of a combination grocery/drug/hardware store, but it also appears that he did some commercial brewing from around 1868 to around 1880. That doesn't surprise local historian Bob Pickett. Bob confirms that "Fall" was a longstanding good name around North Berwick (In fact, it was a Fall - Cappy Fall - who helped save the town from burning down in the Great Fire of 1905.), and then adds: "I imagine there could have been some of that (brewing). There was always something going on." Hard cider, though, was a far bigger commodity. Says Bob: "Mostly there were hard cider people around here. The local farmers got a little extra cash by selling a gallon (of their cider) to anyone who wanted to buy one."

Closing out our list of old-time Maine brewers is Saco. And "The Gateway to Maine" can be proud of its contribution. First came Rumery & Chase, who not only made beer... they made wine as well. They were located at 1 Water Street and were in operation from circa 1868 to circa 1871. John H. Rumery, who was originally from New Hampshire, then exited the scene. But Samuel B. Chase kept on brewing (small beer) and making wine, too. Circa 1876 he, however, called it quits as well.

Saco's next brewing operation took place on the corner of Water and Main streets, where Emery O. Walker made and bottled small beer and soda. An 1872 ad promises "All Orders Promptly Attended To." Walker operated out of his Water and Main facility from 1871 to 1873 or 1874. He then moved his operation to the rear of 79 Main Street and continued to brew until circa 1876. Nothing more is known about him.

There appears to be no still-standing remnant of Saco's brewing past. One Water Street is now the site of a parking lot. Seventy-nine Main Street, on Saco (nee Factory) Island, has been completely leveled.

In addition to those pioneering souls included here, there are quite a few people who are sometimes listed as brewers. They really weren't. They were men who manufactured and sold hop flavored/beerlike "temperance" beverages; i.e., non-alcoholic brews. Chief among these were the Matson brothers, Harris and Louis, who both jointly and individually made and sold "hop beer" in Portland from 1899 until 1920, and (David) Murdock & (Thomas) Freeman, with facilities in Portland and

Ads, 1868-1891, from a trio of Maine's leading hop beer and temperance drink manufacturers of their day. The Hewitts, Frank and Albion, are especially noteworthy. They brewed up "hop, pop & spruce beer" all during the 1860s, 1870s,

STANDARD HOP BEER.

The Great Temperance Drink Appetizer.

MANUFACTURED BY

STANTON & SKINNER,

6 ASH STREET,

Lewiston, ... Maine.

1891

F. E. HEWETT,

Manufacturer of

Soda, Mineral Water, Syrups,

GINGER ALE, HOP, POP & SPRUCE BEER, AND DEALERS IN CIDER.

Ottawa and Cream Beer in Fountains. Soda Fountains Charged.

Corner Main and Rockland Streets, ROCKLAND, ME.

1876

R. ANDERSON & CO.,

MANUFACTURERS OF

BEER OF ALL KINDS,

CORN CAKES, COCOANUT CAKES, CORN BALLS,

SUGARED CORN, SUGARED CORN BALLS.

And also on hand, and for sale wholesale and retail,

Parching Corn, Nuts, Figs, Tobacco, Cigars, Lozenges, and Box Candies of all kinds.

R. Anderson,
J. E. Wallis,   No. 9 Kimball Block, ROCKLAND, Me.
R. Anderson, Jr.

1868

and 1880s. But never the "real thing." In fact, boasted an 1888 article on their operation: "The quality and fineness of flavor of the productions of this house have done more than many a temperance lecture could to assure their general use, and their presence in the community cannot but be productive of good."

Rumford, who made and sold "Ottawa Beer" and "The celebrated UNO Beer" from 1878 until 1918. (Of course "fake beer" had a way of sometimes becoming "real beer." Based on a tip, authorities raided Murdock & Freeman's Portland operation in July of 1901 and, per the Portland *Evening Express*, found "considerable 'straight' beer among the bottles that were supposed to contain nothing stronger than 'UNO' beer." The case was settled out of court.).

Other such "brewers" include: E. Holmes, who made and bottled tonic beer in Springvale for a time around the turn-of-the-century; George H. Winn, who brewed hop beer and Ottawa beer in both Biddeford and Portland from the late 1860s to the late 1870s; Jesse Smith, whose Lancaster Hop Beer Company produced hop beer in Portland from 1890 to 1895; William H. Shaw, who kept Bridgton supplied with hop beer in the mid-1890s; David Hurley, who brewed hop beer in Ellsworth in the mid-1870s; Robert Anderson, who slaked 1860s' and 1870s' Rockland thirsts with hop beer; Albion and Frank Hewitt, who brewed up hop and spruce beer in Rockland from 1860 or so into the late 1880s; Terrence F. Dunn, who provided "soft beer" to parched Bangorites from 1898 until 1906; C.M. Eaton, whose Silver Spring Bottling Works made hop beer in Farmington at the turn of the century; James L. Aggus, who brewed hop beer in Portland in the late 1890s, and last but not least, John McKellar, who turned out hop beer in Thomaston in the 1860s and 1870s.

Photo, May 1995.

Old breweries never die...they just fade away. It's not beautiful.
But it's still standing (or at least it was as of April 1996) and that's
more than can be said for certain for any of Maine's other 19th century brewing operations. This is 118 Main Street in downtown
Auburn. And its basement was home to George E. Kilbourne and
his Crystal Fountain Bottling Co./Kilbourne Bottling Works, brewer
of "All Kinds Of Small Beer" from circa 1890 to circa 1894. Marvel
at the structure while ye may, however, because, sad to say, it's slat-
ed to be torn down.

Anzac, featured here in an August 1918 ad in the
Lewiston Daily Sun, was manufactured by the Anzac
Company (who else?) of Boston, and promoted as
"The Temperance Drink Extraordinary." America -
as well as Maine - would soon be awash in such
cereal beverages and "near beer" brews.

Part II = No Brewers

While there appears to have been very little if any commercial brewing in Maine after 1910, such was not the case across most of the rest of America. Brewing existed; even flourished.

But not for long. The dry juggernaut was sweeping across the land. Fueled by the rhetoric of the W.C.T.U. (Women's Christian Temperance Union) and the Anti-Saloon League, state after state fell into the dry column. The extreme anti-German emotions caused by World War I didn't help, either. After all, names like Schlitz, Anheuser-Busch, Schaefer, Rheingold, Blatz, Pabst, Yuengling, etc., etc. were decidedly German. Things got so bad that the German Brewing Company of Cumberland, Maryland changed its name, in 1917, to the Liberty Brewing Company.

The 18th Amendment

The 18th Amendment to the Constitution – the Prohibition Amendment – was submitted to the states by Congress on December 18, 1917. The first state to ratify it, Mississippi, did so on January 8, 1918. The necessary 36th state (thirty-six was three-quarters of the then 48 states), Nebraska, ratified it on January 16, 1919. Prohibition then became effective and the law of the land one year later, on January 16, 1920. The Volstead (or Prohibition Enforcement) Act was passed by Congress on October 28, 1919. It, too, went into effect on January 16, 1920.

"The Noble Experiment"

On January 16, 1920 – at exactly the stroke of midnight – Maine joined the rest of America in going "dry."

And Maine was not long in joining the rest of America in doing its best to circumvent that dryness.

The "honor" of being the first person to be arrested in Maine for violation of the Volstead Act appears to have gone to one Osmon C. Blaisdell of Lewiston. Or at least so stated *The Lewiston Evening Journal*. Picked up in a Main Street store in Lewiston on January 19th for having "nearly a half a pint of alcohol in his pocket," Blaisdell was described as "quarrelsome." Other early "honorees" included Raymond Clark of Eastport, who was arrested by a customs inspector on January 27th as he attempted to smuggle in four quarts of whiskey via the bridge from Milltown, New Brunswick to Calais, and Oskor H. Aaphi of Bath, who was arrested in Brunswick on the 26th when he showed up to reclaim three-plus gallons of "intoxicating liquor" that had previously been confiscated by Brunswick authorities. Welcome to prohibition!

Other "highlights"– culled from a solid representative sampling of period newspapers from Bangor, Bath, Biddeford, Lewiston and Portland– of the prohibition and "flapper" era in Maine and the nation follow. Some are funny. Some are not. All afford a slice of the 13-year tale of what has become known as "The Noble Experiment."

The thing that made an impression on me was the sense of grand adventure to it all. I suppose being chased and/or shot at isn't really that grand. But, in retrospect anyway, it seems pretty exciting. Rum-running ships, homebrew, buried booze treasure, high-speed auto chases, hidden stills: Maine may not have had Al Capone or Legs Diamond or Eliot Ness but it certainly was not lacking with respect to its prohibition era hoopla and hi-jinks!

1920

VAN BUREN, MARCH 20 - Fifty-eight quarts of whiskey were discovered by customs officials in a snow bank. It is among the first of scores of clever- or not so clever- places Mainers used as "hides" for their beer and booze. Others, before prohibition had run its course, would include: behind a bathtub (Portland, July 1920); in a pickled herring barrel (Waterville, March 1921); under a former pigpen (Portland, March 1921); in an onion bed (Portland, May 1921); in a washtub under the week's wash (Biddeford, July 1922); in a pea patch ("Found Hooch In The Pea-Patch" trumpeted *The Bangor Daily News*; Waldo, July 1922); in shoe boxes (Kennebunk, March 1923); etc. My favorite, though, has to be the hollow leg "hide": in Portland in August 1931 police inspectors found several gallons of booze hidden in the hollow legs of a pair of tables in an apartment on Chatham Street.

PORTLAND, JULY 1 - Schlitz, formerly advertised as "The Beer That Made Milwaukee Famous," is now a near (i.e., non-alcoholic) beer and is advertised as "The Drink That Made Milwaukee Famous."

> Joe: "I see it is predicted we shall
> have a dry and hot summer."
> Moe: "Well, the first part of the
> prophecy is sure to come true."
> Joke, *(Portland) Evening Express*, July 10

BANGOR, AUGUST 4 - "If the moving picture men had been up Hancock Street Wednesday forenoon they might have shot a riot scene that would make fine flavoring for the best of thrillers," wrote *The Bangor Daily News*. That's

America's brewers did not just sit around and let prohibition happen. But they came close to it. Many of them believed, almost to the end, that if prohibition did arrive it would prohibit hard liquor only. As a result, by the time the nation's beer barons got around to flexing some muscle – as with these circa 1917 neck-band messages – it was too late. Prohibition was on the way. And beer was very much included.

PROTEST AGAINST PROHIBITION
THE MORE THE LEGISLATORS HEAR FROM YOU,
THE LESS YOU WILL HEAR OF PROHIBITION.
PROTEST.

OUR ALLIES ARE SOME FIGHTERS
THEIR FIGHTERS AND WORKERS INSIST ON
BEER. WHY TAKE IT AWAY FROM THE LABORING
MEN WHO MUST WIN THE WAR FOR AMERICA?
ASK YOUR LEGISLATORS!

America's first temperance organization of any real significance is generally considered to have been the American Society for the Promotion of Temperance, founded in Boston in 1826. Ninety-four years and many organizations later the "thou shalt not drink" forces of the nation saw their dream come true: prohibition came to the land on January 16, 1920. These sheet music covers, both from 1920, reflect the sentiments of those who did *not* share that dream.

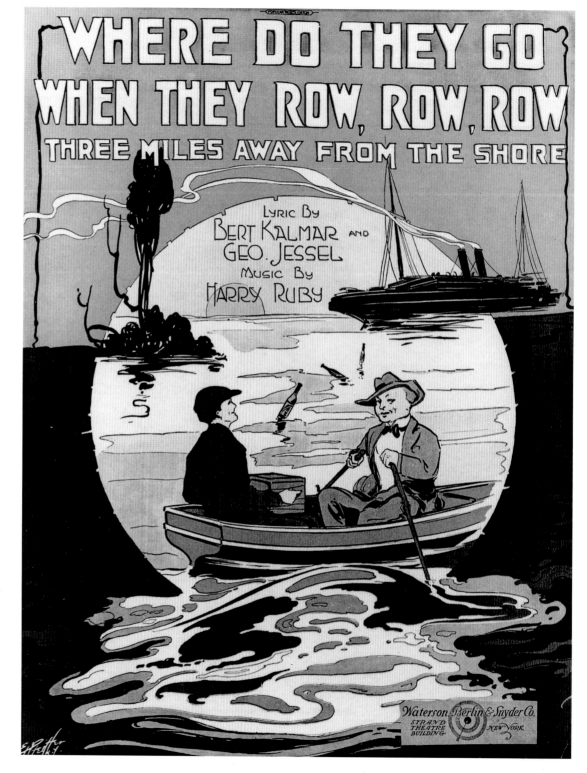

Out past the three-mile limit was international water, where America's prohibition edicts, as this 1920 song lampoons, had no force. The result was (A) a fleet of ships anchored on "Rum Row" that kept smaller and faster craft well stocked with whatever wet stuff they cared to smuggle ashore and (B) a "Booze Cruise" trade that catered to those who wanted to party legally. Three miles out became a very popular spot.

because Simon Taines, "22 and rather audacious," was trying to slip a carload of booze past Sheriff Orman B. Fernandez. He didn't succeed. The Sheriff got wind of it and dispatched two of his best deputies to the scene... and all holy hell broke loose. Simon's mother and a host of neighbors jumped to Simon's aid, refusing to let the deputies search the "booze wagon" and "helping" to unload its contents. An estimated 250 to 500 neighbors "helped out." Finally, Simon decided it was time to beat it. "Right into the crowd plunged the car," wrote the *BDN*. The final tabulation: two people hospitalized and both Simon and his mother charged with a variety of sins. "A full house is expected (when the Taines are arraigned)," signed off the *BDN*, "with a grand time for one and all."

1921

BOSTON, MASS., JAN. 14 - William J. McCarthy, Supervisor of Prohibition Enforcement, announced that $10,000,000 worth of liquor was seized by enforcement agents in New England and New York State (excluding New York City) during the year 1920.

CHICAGO, ILL., JAN. 21 - Noticing that smiles instead of tears were on the faces of visitors to a local undertaking parlor, prohibition agents raided the parlor and found nearly 100 gallons of various liquors hidden in caskets, cupboards, etc.

LISBON FALLS, FEB. 3 - Two hundred cases of "medical tonic" – containing 18% alcohol – were seized by Androscoggin County deputy sheriffs.

MACHIAS, MAY 2 - John Crowe and Simon Bell, both of Bangor, were captured after evading officials at the International Boundary Line at Calais and running through a police barricade in Machias. What finally did them in – and enabled officials to seize the pair's carload of Canadian whiskey – was a draw-bridge that was up.

PORTLAND, JUNE 9 - Cumberland County Sheriff King F. Graham announced that he was going to crack down on druggists who were selling a liniment "rub" that included alcohol as a prominent component: too many people were drinking the "rub."

WASHINGTON, D.C., JULY 1 - Federal Prohibition Commissioner Roy Haynes announced that he was "building up his enforcement army of dry detectives for a new onslaught on bootleggers and enemies of the Volstead Law." He also announced that 100,000 persons had thus far been arrested in the campaign to enforce the law and that he hoped to make the country nearly 100% dry during the next twelve months. "At any rate," he added," we'll make it blamed unpleasant to be a bootlegger."

NEW YORK CITY, N.Y. JULY 4 - Braving brutal humidity and 90° heat, nearly 20,000 marchers paraded up Fifth Avenue in protest of prohibition. Banners were everywhere, and their messages were clear:

> "We are citizens, not inmates."
>
> "The Anti-Saloon League is not run by the brains of the country, but by the hairbrains."
>
> "Only a mother could love a prohibitionist's face."

HOULTON, JULY 6 - After a volley of shots and a high-speed chase in dense fog, three Aroostook County deputy sheriffs overtook a carload of six rum-runners near here. A pitched hand-to-hand battle ensued until, outnumbered two to one, the deputies were beaten off and the rum-runners sped away. The deputies took chase again, only to be foiled again. The rum-running six managed to tear up a small bridge and, as the United Press rather graphically described it: "The deputies' machine, speeding along in the dense fog, struck the open bridge, catapulted through the air and landed on the side of the road." The deputies, miraculously, escaped injury. The rum-runners got away.

EASTPORT, JULY 9 - Tom Cameron of Eastport was shot twice in the hip by law enforcement officials who claimed to be after 300 quarts of whiskey thought to be smuggled in from New Brunswick by motorboat. Cameron claimed he was "standing by the roadside when officers in two cars approached and commenced firing" at him.

NEW YORK CITY, N.Y., JULY 25 - Federal officials admitted that many Atlantic Coast fishermen were substituting rum-running for fishing. "Reaping a rich harvest running the forbidden cargoes ashore, they work almost entirely at night, making landings at points known to be free from surveillance," ran an article in the *Evening Express*, continuing "The smugglers are met on shore by automobile truckmen who whisk the cargoes away to secret storehouses."

WASHINGTON, D.C., OCT. 24 - The Internal Revenue Service issued regulations which allowed beer to be prescribed as a medicine. A physician could henceforth prescribe up to a case of beer if he/she felt it was beneficial to

Here's how the girls of Chi Gamma Theta sorority lined up for their photograph in the *Colby Oracle* (yearbook) for 1921. The question is: are those bottles of brew lined up with them? Maybe yes. Maybe no. Either way, it's a wonderful photo.

a patient's health. Written into the regulations was a provision that prohibited the doctor from writing a prescription for beer for himself/herself.

1922

MINNEAPOLIS, MINN., JAN. 9 - Federal agents seized 200 "customized" coconuts – each had been hollowed out and filled with a pint of strong Jamaica rum – at a Minneapolis railway station.

BATH, JAN. 11 - Sagadahoc County Sheriff Wilbur Oliver and federal officials smashed an alleged rum-running ring centered in Bath. In what *The Lewiston Daily Sun* headlined a "Sensational Liquor Escapade In Bath," two men and their liquor-laden brand-new Stutz sedan were captured after an exchange of gunfire on Pine Street. Another man and a woman got away.

BUTTE, MONT., JAN. 25 - Sewers on the east side of this city were blocked by large deposits of homebrew and moonshine mash. Included in the melange were prune seeds, rice, barley and corn residue, raisins, and cherry pits.

BOSTON, MASS., APRIL 17 - A *Boston Globe* survey of 14 leading New England cities showed a steady increase in crime. Authorities blamed unemployment, the lingering effects of the World War... and prohibition. "The Volstead Act, its failure of enforcement and the general contempt with which it is viewed by the public" is how the survey phrased it.

ELLSWORTH, MAY 17 - Federal officials raided the home of Dr. Alexander C. Haggerthy, former long-time Ellsworth mayor, where they found a huge cache of whiskey, gin, and beer. As *The Bangor Daily News*, which knew how to have fun with prohibition doings, put it: "They (the Feds) went to Ellsworth dry and light and came back at night with four truckloads of the best liquors that the Demon had succeeded in keeping under cover in this part of the world." Further reflected the *BDN*: "The sight of so much good stuff going into dry slavery (in the basement of the Bangor Custom House) moved many an epicure to tears."

SKOWHEGAN, MAY 28 - Somerset County Judge J. Deasy ruled, in the State of Maine vs. Edward Sayers, that rose water, containing 50% alcohol, is most definitely an intoxicating beverage.

A man's cellar is being searched by a prohibition enforcement officer.

"There are hundreds and hundreds
of empty beer bottles down here,"
the officer says. "How did they
get here, friend?"
"Darned if I know," answers the man,
"I've never bought an empty beer
bottle in my life."
    1922 joke

VERONA, JUNE 16 - In an article headlined "Booze Hide In A Verona Barn," *The Bangor Daily News* again had some fun. Wrote they: "Federal Enforcement Officer Robert Jack and some of his merry men went on a tour of exploration Friday morning, heading down through Bucksport to the Verona bridge, then across and far down the island where nobody lives. Coming to an abandoned farm they turned in through the bushes and tall grass and came to an old barn. In the barn, strange to say, the federal men found 53 cases of whiskey, five cases of gin and a case of vermouth. While the officers were there a man drove up in a Packard touring car. He didn't know Jack or Jack's men – may have thought they were some of the natives. In the course of conversation he said he had 'come after the rest of the stuff.' The man, who proved to be Capt. James E. Collins of St. John, N.B., skipper of the motor boat Lilly, which was anchored in Bucksport harbor at the time, was placed under arrest. Just about that time Pope D. McKinnon and his son happened along, a mere incident of course, Mr. McKinnon no doubt being down there for a few clams. The McKinnons, at the invitation of Mr. Jack, joined the party and all hands and the booze came to Bangor." (Ed. note: No connection with the case could be shown and the McKinnons were not held.).

FORT FAIRFIELD, JULY 25 - The Boundary Hotel, located partly in the U.S. and partly in Canada, was raided by U. S. Customs officials. The officials found 132 quarts of ale, much to the chagrin of the hotel's management, on the American side.

RUMFORD, DEC. 9 - People wondered how Pete Morrell could always have a "Fresh Clams Today" sign tacked up in front of his Oxford Avenue restaurant. In season and out of season. The answer was revealed when prohibition agents raided Pete's place and found that barrels that supposedly held clams were barrels that held booze as well. When opened, the barrels contained about a peck of clams covering a dozen or so one-gallon cans of wine.

1923

"A federal court has just ruled that cider is not a soft drink. Probably anybody who has ever experienced the morning after effects of an evening of close communion with a cask of two year old cider will be in full agreement with the court decision."

Joke, *Biddeford Daily Journal,* Jan. 11

BIDDEFORD, MARCH 27 - A "suggestive gurgle" was the undoing of two men who gave their names as Tony Valouch and Sam Loyminos and claimed to be Rumford mill workers. The men were arrested by a Boston & Maine police lieutenant after he'd noticed a pair of trunks in the baggage car that, when moved, gave out with the telltale gurgle. Sixteen gallons of "the stuff that inebriates," as the *Biddeford Daily Journal* worded it, was found hidden in the trunks.

CHICAGO, ILL., MAY 22 - The *Chicago Daily News* declared that an army of 25,000 smugglers was bringing over 100,000 gallons of Canadian liquor and beer into the U.S. each and every day. One federal prohibition enforcement officer was quoted as saying "I don't believe a fifty foot wall along the entire Canadian line would make them (the smugglers) stop."

SACO, JULY 1 - York County Deputy Sheriffs Charles E. Clark and Henry A. Berube seized 173 cases of ale at Bugbee and Brown Co., a wholesaler located at 28 Washington Street. The company's manager, Michael J. Boland, expressed surprise when the haul tested at between five and six percent alcohol, stating that he had "supposed the ale contained not more than one half of one per cent of alcohol."

VANCEBORO, DEC. 4 - A boxcar loaded with "sardines" was seized by customs officials. The car contained 807 crates. Of these, 307 did contain sardines. The other 500 contained liquor, a dozen bottles to the crate. Whiskey was the "sardine" of choice: there were 485 crates of whiskey, with the rest a mix of wine and gin.

> Farmer: "Have the cows all been milked?"
> Farm hand: "All but the American one."
> Farmer: "Which one is the American one?"
> Farm hand: "The one that's gone dry."
> British joke, 1923

1924

LUBEC, APRIL 4 - *The Bangor Daily News* reported, seemingly in earnest, that "Anti-Freeze Cocktails are the latest drink favored by those whose stomachs have hitherto stood the acid test of modern prohibition beverages." No less an authority than Lubec's "Mike, the Clam Shocker" is quoted: "Take a quart of anti-freeze, mix it with a bottle of ginger ale and shake it a little. Let it set in the sun a while to get the hydraulic acid out of it, then shake it some more, and try it. Wait a minute after the first drink. If it don't kill yer, take another one and so on." Incidentally, Mike had harsh words for anyone imbibing canned heat: that stuff, he said flat out, "is sure to ruin their stomach."

WISCASSET, JUNE 5 - While searching for goods stolen in a series of minor break-ins in the area, Wiscasset officers stumbled upon a still on Goose Island in the Sheepscot River. And it was in perfect working order for the manufacture of whiskey. Taken into custody were Nathan Pushard, 16, and Lee Nichols, 17.

BANGOR, JUNE 6 - In what was called "The Eastport Whiskey-Sardine Conspiracy Case," five people were indicted by a federal grand jury. The indictment contained a rather involved list of 21 "overt acts." The basics, though, were that the defendants, headed by one Charles A. Haydock of Eastport, allegedly transported 800 cases of sardines from Lubec to some point in the Bay of Fundy where they were met by a motorboat from St. Stephen, New Brunswick loaded with liquor, and the liquor was packed in the sardine cans for shipment through Canada to Cleveland, Ohio.

1925

KITTERY, MARCH 13 - "Ford Of Ancient Origin - Liquor Of Recent Vintage" ran the (Portland) *Evening Express* story. It told the tale of Anthony Rossi of Portland, a bootlegger with an antique set of wheels... a vintage Ford so old prohibition agents were uncertain of its age. But "roped and wired together," Anthony's vehicle and Anthony were making a run from Boston to Portland with a cargo of 30 gallons of booze when they were stopped, not by mechanical failure, but by the arm of the law. Rossi was arrested and his car, as was the case with all cars and trucks used for rum-running, was confiscated. Commented the *Evening Express:* "There is little likelihood that bidding will be spirited when it (Rossi's auto) is put up at auction along with other seized vehicles."

Today we call it NA or non-alcoholic beer. But in days of old, as with this circa 1922 postcard, beer with less than ½ of 1% alcohol was known as "near beer." And it was not loved. As one social commentator of the day wrote: "The man who called it 'near beer' was a bad judge of distance."

"Same old bar and the same old feet
In the same old place in the same old street;
Same old pose on the same old rail,
Same old drink? Shucks, ginger ale!"
    1925 rhyme

LIMESTONE, AUG. 22 - Rather than give himself and the 500 bottles of beer and whiskey he was carrying up to authorities, Adelord Brissette drove 18 miles even though shot in the arm. It happened when Brissette and his partner, Leo Voisin, were motoring through Caswell, about ten miles from Limestone. A contingent of border patrol and customs agents tried to stop the duo but Adelord had other plans: he speeded up, almost running over one of the agents. The agent opened fire, hitting Brissette in his left arm. Brissette's stoicism, however, was of no avail: the agents tracked him down at his home in Caribou and both he and Voisin were taken into custody.

BANGOR, AUG. 8 - A boxcar filled with Canadian ale – 10,000 22-ounce bottles worth! – was seized by law enforcement agents north of Bangor. The car was part of a Bangor & Aroostook freight bound for Northeast Maine Junction. Penobscot County Sheriff John K. Farrar said he was not sure of the cargo's supposed destination, but believed it was "intended for New England or trade further west."

BERWICK, AUG. 12 - Arraigned for having three kegs of wine and a half a barrel of beer in her possession, Mrs. George Howarth of Berwick pleaded not guilty, that it was all for "medicinal purposes." And she had evidence to that fact. And she was released.

1926

BRUNSWICK, MAY 6 - In a study conducted in association with the National Student Federation of America, 140 out of 220 students polled at Bowdoin said they favored a change in the prohibition law. Of the 140, 96 (68%) were in favor of allowing beer and light wines, while 44 (32%) were for total repeal.

ROCHESTER, N.Y., MAY 7 - Professor Frank M. Keith's sweet dreams of riches (or dreams of sweet riches!) were dashed following a raid on his home by federal agents. A large quantity of caramels, each containing one ounce of whiskey, was seized.

SOUTH PORTLAND, JUNE 30 - While searching for stolen tires at the residence of James H. Cribbey on School Street, police officers found 16 one-gallon containers of newly-made homebrew and 20 quarts of beer. They also found the tires.

WINDHAM, JULY 30 - "Hay" and "hard cider" were one and the same to a select few in Windham, according to Cumberland County Deputy Sheriff Frank L. Baker. He arrested Harlon A. Sayward of Windham after twice visiting Sayward's home out of uniform and purchasing "hay" by the gallon. "Got any hay left?" he asked. Sayward smiled and asked a few questions of his own before being satisfied that Baker was okay and hadn't just stumbled upon the password. The "hay" was $2.00 a gallon and tested out at 6% alcohol.

BRIDGEPORT, CONN., AUGUST 5 - Walter Stanton, 22, and William J. Lockwood, 40, who were driving a truck filled with bootleg beer, made the mistake of driving it into a Connecticut State Police car being driven by two Connecticut State Policemen. Suspicious of such reckless driving, the state troopers searched the truck and were rewarded with the discovery of 20 half barrels of illegal beer.

PORTLAND, AUG. - OCT. - The (Portland) *Evening Express* dubbed it "The Celebrated Syrup-Malt Case." The three defendants, all downtown Portland grocery store proprietors, called it hogwash. The three were arrested August 12th, charged with doing an extensive business selling malt syrup to be used in the manufacture of beer "with a kick to it." The defendants contended they had no way of knowing what purchasers were using the syrup for. After several continuances, one of which was worth a big and bold front page "Syrup-Malt Case Continued Again" headline in the *Express* of September 3rd, the three proprietors were found not guilty by Judge C. W. Peabody on October 21st on the grounds of insufficient evidence.

PORTLAND, OCT. 9 - When Cumberland County Sheriff King F. Graham and his men arrested Alfred Herregoldts of Medford, Mass. near the Willowdale Golf Links in Portland they were in for a surprise. As the man who Sheriff Graham had named "Portland's Society Bootlegger" was being searched, out popped a wallet containing a list of many of Portland's prominent citizens. Herregoldts readily admitted these were patrons of his, patrons to whom he had delivered many a bottle of champagne and/or Scotch and/or rye. The list, according to the (Portland) *Evening Express*, read like a "page from Who's Who in Portland". The Sheriff said he might take steps to arrest the guilty members of the city's "Smart Set."

1927

LONDON, ENGLAND, JAN. 6 - "Beer is better for the health than tea or coffee because of its vitamin content": so said Dr. J. Lewis Rosedale of St. Thomas' Hospital in an address before the People's League of Health on the topic of common errors of diet. Rosedale said beer contains vitamin B and possesses a large dietetic value. He termed both tea and coffee "valueless."

"A Biddeford cocktail consists of
a combination of cod liver oil and
alcohol, where the imbiber has to
press a straw down two or three inches
in the oil in order to reach the
second content. But even a Biddeford
toper would want to be sure the straw
didn't leak."
(Portland) *Evening Express*, May 4

VANCEBORO, MAY 4 - Noticing that some of the bags "gurgled," customs inspectors examined a boxcar load of "potatoes" and discovered booze among the spuds. Of the 547 bags of so-called potatoes, 247 contained whiskey or gin, a dozen bottles to a bag. The load had been on its way from Gagetown, P.E.I. to Woonsocket, R.I. Instead it ended up at the Custom House in Portland.

"Yeast is yeast, and hops are hops,
And ever the twain shall meet
In the brewer's vat and the home-brew pot
While the Congressman sleeps in his seat."
Edward Little High School (Auburn) yearbook, *The Oracle*, May

PORTLAND, JUNE 6 - Evangelist Billy Sunday spoke before an audience of 2,000 at City Hall and declared that "We are rearing a generation of moonshine, bootlegging, jazzing, joy riding children who will suffer from the sins of parents and become the worst types of juvenile criminals. They are conceived by drunken parents and born amidst home brew environment."

CAMBRIDGE, MASS., JUNE 7 - "White Mule," a bootleg liquor with a lot of "kick," caused an avalanche of excitement in Judge Arthur P. Stone's district courtroom. "With the rattle of artillery fire, 250 bottles and five gallon cans blew up as a police sergeant was testifying against Joseph Rivers, owner of the 'White Mule.' Judge Stone dodged behind his robes, lawyers ran from the bar and prisoners in the dock and spectators sought shelter as the entire courtroom was showered with the liquor." As for Rivers, he was fined $500 and sentenced to six months in jail. He appealed.

CHICAGO, ILL., JUNE 1 - One-hundred and one citizens of Melrose Park were indicted by a Federal Grand Jury for alleged moonshining. Included were the village's mayor and a trustee. The government charged there were 119 operating stills in the village, a suburb of Chicago with a population of 10,000.

TO A FELLOW~SUFFERER

WHERE DO WE GO FROM HERE, BOYS?
WWHERE DO WE GO FROM HERE?
FOR THEY'VE CALLED A HALT ON THE HOP AND MALT-
IT'S NIX ON THE GOOD OLD BEER:
IT'S NIX ON THE OLD RYE HIGHBALL-
WITH A GOOD SONG RINGING CLEAR-
IT'S A———— OF A NOTE FOR A THIRSTY THROAT-
SAY! WHERE DO WE GO FROM HERE?

By 1922, approximately when these "lamentatory" postcards were printed, prohibition was about as much in place as it would ever be. On March 9th of that year New Jersey became the 46th and last state to ratify the 18th Amendment. Connecticut and Rhode Island never did ratify it... but they had to live with it anyway.

No, it's not Bangor or Caribou or Fryeburg. It's not even North America. It's the cover photo for a 1924 article on Scotland Yard's use of radio in crime detection. But you may be certain that America's prohibition agents utilized radio police cars – along with searchplanes, armed cars, Coast Guard cutters, high-powered motor trucks and just about anything and everything else that moved – in their war against the nation's army of rum-runners.

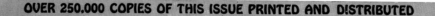

OVER 250,000 COPIES OF THIS ISSUE PRINTED AND DISTRIBUTED

RADIO NEWS

REG. U.S. PAT. OFF.

25 Cents
January
1924
Over 200 Illustrations

Edited by H. GERNSBACK

THE RADIO POLICE CAR

See Page 870

IN THIS ISSUE

Lieut. Col. J. O. Mauborgne
Capt. H. W. Webbe
Dr. Albert Neuburger
John L. Reinartz, 1 QP

XB-71

THE 100% WIRELESS MAGAZINE

CIRCULATION LARGER THAN ANY OTHER RADIO PUBLICATION

PORTLAND, JUNE 20 - Two jail sentences for drinking were meted out in Municipal Court by Judge Max L. Pinansky. The Judge had a way with words. The first defendant promised he would stop drinking and get a job "as soon as the weather clears up." "Ten days in jail," the Judge ruled, continuing "It will probably be clear by then." Defendant number two, a seaman, promised he would be leaving port the next Thursday as that's when his ship would be sailing . "Ten days in jail," was the Judge's response again, adding "I guess you won't take that ship."

> Chuck: I thought you promised
> to save me some of that home brew
> you had."
> Wally: "Well, I tried to, but it ate holes
> through everything I put it in and
> so I finally had to drink it."
> 1927 joke

WEST STERLING, MASS., JULY 27 - "Tipsy chickens staggering around the yard as a result of eating moonshine mash" were found, according to the Associated Press, by state policemen who raided the farm of John Katinas and seized 650 gallons of mash, 150 gallons of finished moonshine, a 100-gallon still in operation, and an automobile alleged to be used to transport the moonshine.

> "Mother's in the kitchen
> Washing out the jugs;
> Sister's in the pantry
> Bottling the suds;
> Father's in the cellar
> Mixing up the hops;
> Johnny's on the front porch
> Watching for the cops."
> 1928 rhyme

WASHINGTON, D.C., NOV. 6 - In the presidential election, Al Smith, running on a "wet" platform, is trounced by incumbent Herbert Hoover. In Maine, Smith, the Democrat, captures but three of the state's 20 cities. The three are Biddeford, Lewiston, and Waterville.

1929

PORTLAND, JAN. 1 - Speaking at a New Year's Eve ser-vice at the Second Parish Congregational Church, Judge Max L. Pinansky congratulated the attendees... and scolded New Year's revelers. Said the Judge: "Men in full dress suits and women in almost undress suits, hilariously romping up and down hotel corridors, roadhouses, dance halls and in private homes, becoming more and more inebriated from poisonous liquors, are in no condition to know what the New Year is all about."

NEW YORK CITY, N.Y., JAN. 1 - In offering a $25,000 cash prize for the best plan to remedy the evils of prohibition, William Randolph Hearst – previously an avid dry – states: "I think it can be truthfully said today that any man who wants a drink can get one; and about the only difference between the present condition and the condition preceding prohibition is that a man who wants a mild drink is compelled to take a strong one; and a man who wants a good drink is compelled to take a bad one."

> Stranger: "Do you have to see a doctor
> before you get liquor in this town?
> Native: "Nope. Afterward."
> Joke, *The Bangor Daily News*, May 7

SKOWHEGAN, JULY 5 - When Somerset County deputy sheriffs raided the camp of Joseph Smith in Moscow (Maine) the night of July 3rd they found 35 gallons of beer. In court, Smith pleaded not guilty; that he only drank the beer because "the water is so poor." Trial Justice John H. Lancaster fined Smith $100.00 and costs.

PORTLAND, SEPT. 6 - A day in court brought attention to "Portland's latest cocktail"... a bay rum straight. It seems that bay rum – with a 50% alcohol content! – had suddenly become a hot seller in a number of the Forest City's drug and chain stores. "The 10 cent jag"– it cost but a dime a bottle – is how imbibers described the effect of bay rum to Municipal Court Judge Max L. Pinansky. The Judge issued a warning that the continued indiscriminate sale of the liquid in question would result in prosecution in court.

> "Who is that man the crowd is chasing?"
> "He's a bootlegger."
> "Going to mob him?"
> "No, trying to get the first chance to do
> business with him."
> Joke, *Bangor Daily News*, Oct. 2

NEW YORK CITY, N.Y., OCT. 29 - The Stock Market crashed. While spelling financial disaster to the country as a whole, the crash – and the Depression it signaled – turned out to be beneficial to the "Bring Back Beer" movement.

1930

PORTLAND, JAN. 3 - Municipal Court Judge Max L. Pinansky handed out a $200.00 fine and two months in jail to Mrs. Pearl St. Germain. Mrs. St. Germain had been arrested after authorities found 27 quart bottles of beer and 14 gallons of mash in her home on Oxford Street. Questioned by the judge as to who drank the beer, Mrs. Germain said that she did, and explained that she had been told it was good for her health. She further explained that "All of the grocery stores sell it (beer), or at least the malt to make it." In rendering his decision, Judge Pinansky stated: "I don't take stock in the story of any woman who drinks liquor."

NEW YORK CITY, N.Y., JAN. 16 - On this, the tenth anniversary of prohibition, William Randolph Hearst again spoke out: "Prohibition has made our president a dictator, executing an unpopular law by force of arms. It has made our congressmen cowards and hypocrites, passing more and oppressive laws, while themselves carrying whisky flasks in their hip pockets. Prohibition has divided our people into factions almost as bitterly hostile to each other as the factions that existed before the Civil War."

PORTLAND, MAY 5 - Judge Max L. Pinansky struck again when, in Municipal Court, he ruled that it is indiscreet and improper for a person to drink near beer and then get behind the wheel of a car... stating his belief that near beer, even though considered non-alcoholic and perfectly legal, was capable of upsetting the stomach and thereby getting a person in such a frame of mind that he/she might not be capable of driving. In hearing the case against a motorist named Donald Grant, 27, of Danforth Street, the judge listened as Grant said he had consumed several bottles of a near beer named Valley Forge (ed. note: Valley Forge was a product of Adam Scheidt, Norristown, Pa.) before taking the wheel and being involved in an accident. "That (Valley Forge) is a patriotic name," declared the judge, "but I'm afraid if they drank that at Valley Forge we wouldn't have the success in this country that we have had."

Modern version of old proverb:
"Eat, drink and be merry, for
tomorrow your bootlegger may be
caught."
    Joke, *The Bangor Daily News*, July 3

SUMTER, S.C., OCT. 3 - The Great Depression hit even the moonshine trade. That was evidenced recently when Sumter officers located a still. Every utensil of the well-equipped liquor maker was on hand, but there was no mash or no operators in sight. Then the officers noticed a sign on a nearby tree. It read: "Closed on account of the hard times."

"Americanism: Arresting men for
possessing beer-making equipment
with which to break the law; making
a selling point of a car's ability to
break all speed laws."
    (Portland) *Evening Express*, Nov. 12

1931

The bootlegger was recommending a brand
of rum he offered for sale.
"Jamaica?," inquired the prospect.
"No, I didn't make it," replied the
bootlegger.
    (Portland) *Evening Express*, Jan. 1

PORTLAND, MAY 4 - Cumberland County Deputy Sheriff Guilford F. Pendexter got the ride of his life – and almost his death – early tonight on the running board of a "new roadster." Pendexter had spotted the roadster and rum-running suspects James Sowers of Houghton and Thomas J. Maley of Portland as they stopped for a red light at Longfellow Square. Jumping out of his own car, Pendexter leaped upon the running board of the roadster and demanded the duo stop. Instead they leadfooted the accelerator, racing top speed down State Street and then onto Grant Street, all the while punching and pushing Pendexter as he held on for dear life. Finally, in desperation, the deputy managed to draw his revolver and send a bullet through Sowers' leg and into Maley's foot. That brought the roadster to a screeching halt... and Pendexter got his men.

BOOTLEG BEN

Bootleg Ben was a square old guy
Who filled his jugs with good red-eye,
But Friday last was hard on Ben
And now he sleeps in Thomaston Pen.

"It happened this way," the runner sighed,
"My Packard's engine suddenly died
With the sheriff's car right on my track—
I'd grazed a cop by just a crack."

"I jumped out and tried to run
While the sheriff pulled his big six-gun.
He shouted, 'Halt!' as loud as that
And neatly drilled my new felt hat."

Ben hired a lawyer, the best of men
To keep him out of Thomaston Pen.
The lawyer roared and did his best,
But Ben became a government guest.

"Ten years," quoth the judge and nodded his
    head
While Bootleg Ben almost fell dead.
"I'll get a pardon" the lawyer shouted,
But the poor man's argument was flouted.

Remember good and better men,
What happend to poor Bootleg Ben.
And when you're making poor home-brew,
You may be caught by the sheriff too.

———————

Poem, *The Academy Review*,
student magazine of Foxcroft Academy,
Dover-Foxcroft, May, 1924

These are two in a series of "If Only It Were Beer" postcards published in Great Britain, probably in the late-to-mid 1920s. Were our British cousins having fun at our expense? It's likely. They certainly did find prohibition quite amusing. As long as it didn't find its way to their shores.

The Stein Song

The *Stein Song* is relatively close to 100 years old. That's a lot of steins! The tune that would become the University of Maine song was created in 1904. And, not surprisingly, it was created at the University of Maine. According to historian Parker B. Albee, Jr., writing in the *Maine Sunday Telegram* in June 1988, the song was the product of two rich and fertile minds embodied in undergraduate room-mates Lincoln Colcord and Adelbert Sprague. Sprague was taken with a march song that had been written by one Emil Fenstad in 1901. He thought his roommate might be just the man to put words to the song, originally entitled *Opie*. He was right. Colcord, probably more as a lark than for any other reason, took the sheet music for the march to the university's music room and composed a set of words while tinkling out the melody on a piano. So enthused did he become that he cut both of his morning's classes. It was worth it: when Colcord saw Sprague later in the day he was able to unveil the highly charged "Fill the steins to dear old Maine! / Shout 'til the rafters ring! / Stand and drink the toast once again! / Let ev'ry loyal Maine man sing" lyrics that have inspired countless legions since.

The *Stein Song*, however, was not an instant hit. The words were far from a favorite of many on campus. At first, in fact, the "liquid" nature of the song's lyrics caused it to be banned by a faculty screening committee. But Colcord and Sprague persisted, finally going directly to the top, to university president George E. Fellows. Fellows agreed with the faculty committee: he knew a drinking song when he heard one. "But," he reasoned as he gave the song his blessing, "now that we have prohibi-tion (in Maine) one can only drink milk or water any-way." One may only assume that the good president winked as he spoke those hallowed words.

Fill The Steins To Dear Old Rudy

The *Stein Song* became, in due course, the official University of Maine song. But it took Rudy Vallée to make it a national hit. That happened in 1929-1930. Rudy, who'd been raised in Westbrook and even attended UMO

for a time, was at the peak of his very considerable popu-larity. His weekly radio program, broadcast nationally from New York City, was heard by millions. Adelbert Sprague, by then head of the university's music depart-ment, decided to chance sending a copy of the song to Rudy in the hope he might sing it on his show. And that's just what Rudy did... catapulting it to national – and international – bestseller status almost overnight.

Fill The Steins To Dear Old Adelbert And Lincoln

The *Stein Song* is hardly a top 40 hit nowadays. Neither Janet Jackson nor Aerosmith is rushing to record it. But it's still the University of Maine song. How many times has the song been sung? Who knows. How many touch-downs has Maine scored since 1904? How many alumni gatherings have been held? How many old – and young – Maine grads have hummed it as they've walked down the street?

Fill the steins to the dear old *Stein Song*.

Dick Hubsch
Carmel, New York

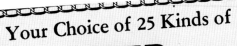

Your Choice of 25 Kinds of
BEER

TO TAKE OUT

MAHON'S

Telephone 414-2

The place to take your
friends to eat or for
a refreshing
drink

LUCHINI'S
MAIN ST., ELLSWORTH

**GOOD MUSIC
GOOD BEER
GOOD FUN**

AT

JO'S SANDWICH SHOP

Cottage St., Bar Harbor
NEWSPAPERS   MAGAZINES

All three of these ads are
from an April 1930 issue of a
slim little newspaper called
the *Ellsworth Daily Times.* It's
amazing how all three certainly look and sound as if
they were for the "real
thing." But they weren't.

"The election now is all over
And died away is the cheer
And now we only are waiting
To see when we will get beer
                Rhyme, (Portland) *Evening Express*, Nov. 9

CHICAGO, NOV. 10 - Confident that the nation's sweeping endorsement of FDR insures the speedy re-legalization of beer, midwestern brewers announced they were ready to reopen and enlarge their plants and put thousands of people back to work. Mayor Anton J. Cermak of Chicago expressed his opinion that, when back, the foamy beverage should retail for 5 cents a glass and 10 cents a stein.

1933

By 1933 the mood of Maine – and the nation – was far different with respect to beer and booze than had been the case from 1920 through

1932. Rumrunning and illicit still and home brew seizures slowed down. That beer was coming back was almost a certainty, and both wets and drys jockeyed back and forth as to what strength it should be: i.e, what percentage of alcohol was intoxicating and what strength wasn't.

Representative Ernest J. Audet of Lewiston got Maine off and running on the return-of-beer issue when, on January 12th, he introduced a bill providing for the sale and transportation of beer having an alcoholic content not greater than that to be established by the federal government. Detractors chided Audet about being in a rush; that it would make more sense to wait

By the early 1930s the American economy was in bad shape. Many people believed that beer could help. On the reverse side of this circa 1931 postcard is the message: "I favor modification of the Volstead Act, permitting the manufacture of beer... thus providing direct and indirect employment to a vast army of workers, helping the farmer and enriching the U.S. Treasury with revenue now lost, restoring public confidence and stimulating all business." Recipients were urged to mail ten or more of the cards to friends and acquaintances in order to "Spread the Doctrine of Prosperity."

Sheet music cover, 1933. When beer and wine of a modest 3.2% strength became legal again in the spring/summer of 1933 most of America rejoiced. Many rejoiced even more when, in December, the 18th (Prohibition) Amendment was overturned by the necessary three-quarters of the states. Hard liquor – as well as beer and wine of greater than 3.2% – then became fully legal... except, of course, where prohibited by state or local statute. Maine was in the latter category: it did not allow the sale of hard liquor and "high power" beer until November of 1934.

until the Feds had given beer a definite green light. Audet's response: "You can buy alcohol anywhere in the State of Maine for $3.00 a gallon." His bill, he made clear, was a temperance bill, a bill that was "badly needed."

Audet's bill failed. But legal beer was not to be denied. In Washington, FDR was sworn in as the 32nd president on March 4th. Unemployment was estimated at over 12,000,000, and 45,000,000 Americans were said to be living in poverty. FDR wasted little time. Visualizing the return of beer as a giant step toward happier days he, on March 13th, issued a brief – it was but two sentences long – message to Congress strongly urging the immediate legalization of beer. The message read: "I recommend to the Congress the passage of legislation for the immediate modification of the Volstead Act in order to legalize the manufacture and sale of beer and other beverages of such alcoholic content as is permissible under the Constitution; and to provide through such manufacture and sale, by substantial taxes, a proper and much-needed revenue for the government. I deem action at this time to be of the highest importance."

Congress, too, wasted little time. The Senate voted yes to the return of beer on March 20th. The House followed suit the very next day, on the 21st. FDR certainly didn't dawdle, either: he signed the bill, legalizing 3.2% beer and wine as of midnight on April 6th, on the 22nd. Looking up as he signed the bill, the president smiled and told the photographers present that he hoped they "got the smile."

Meanwhile, back in Maine a beer bill was again on the move. The state Senate okeyed a return-of-brew bill on March 23rd; the House gave its approval on March 28th; Governor Louis J. Brann made it official by signing the bill a few minutes before noon on the 29th.

At the stroke of midnight on April 6th – often called "New Beer's Eve" – twenty states and the District of Columbia celebrated the return of legal beer. It was a festive event! As the Associated Press reported, "Enough beer went down the hatch in the United States to float a battleship." And, added the AP, "If breweries had been able to supply all demands they could have sold enough to have floated two battleships." Maine, alas, was not part of the party. But it soon would be: its beer bill called for the legal sale of brew as of midnight on June 30th.

Beer, Beer, Beer Makes Maine Want To Cheer, Cheer, Cheer

May and June of 1933 were exciting months in the Pine Tree State. It was not just because a golden amber beverage was going to be (legally) back in the picture. It was because, to many, its return signaled the hope of something even better than beer... prosperity. And that signal could not have come at a more opportune time: Ellsworth and the New Auburn section of Auburn both suffered disastrous fires in May; Presque Isle and neighboring Washburn were paying creditors with script money; bank failures – both rumored and actual – were rife throughout the state.

So beer was a perk. People in Lewiston seemed

to especially have fun with it. In late April the *Lewiston Evening Journal* sent a reporter to Massachusetts – where beer had just become legal – to report on the happenings. Just over the state line from New Hampshire the reporter was greeted with a roadside restaurant where "hot dogs and cold bottles (of beer) were keeping a big crew busy." The reporter quickly discovered, however, that the restaurant's patrons weren't too happy. "No kick" was the major complaint. A little investigative reporting led to the finding that the weakness of the new beer – compared to home brew – was a complaint throughout the Bay State. In fact, a Boston newspaper had enlisted two of its staff to each drink a case – 24 full bottles! – of the new brew... and then go on the air over a local radio station and report how they felt. They did fine... which said quite a bit in itself. As the Lewiston scribe duly reported: "A case of beer in the old days and they (the Boston duo) would have got the air all right... but not to broadcast over." Another highlight was a Lewiston Gas Light Company ad for what they dubbed "The 3.2 Refrigerator." The name came from the legal limit – 3.2% alcohol by volume – established by Congress and soon to be in place in Maine. The refrigerator, an Air-Cooled Electrolux model, came out just as FDR was signing the beer bill and featured what was described as a split shelf "to permit the housing of a case of 24 bottles" of the new brew. Bradford, Conant and Company, located at 199-203 Lisbon Street, advertised a 7-piece beer set – a pitcher and six mugs – with a headline that read "You'll Surely Need Them Now." And last, two of Lewiston's finest – Chief John H. Ashton and Capt. Picard – took a two-day spin through New Hampshire and Massachusetts, where beer had already made its comeback, to better learn how to deal with "the beer situation." The *Evening Journal* reported the pair made the trip in the department's brand new Ford V-8.

In Bangor, ads that promised "Beer Won't Make You Fat" (for a weight-reduction program called the Vannay Treatment) and that encouraged farmers to plant barley appeared in the *Bangor Daily News*. Even a "What Suds!" ad for Rinso Soap appeared to be in the spirit of things. Meanwhile, in Augusta, Maine's guiding lights pinned down what was to be allowed. "An Act Relating To Malt Beverages and To Derive Revenue From the Manufacture and Sale Thereof" was passed by the legislature on April 26th. Malt beverages were defined as "all non-intoxicating beverages containing malt and containing more than ½ of 1 percent of alcohol by volume." The date set for the legal sale of such malt beverages was midnight of June 30th (i. e., July 1st).

"It'll Be Here In Oceans"

By the last week in June everything was in place for beer's triumphant day in Maine. Over 1,500 malt beverage licenses had been granted throughout the state. Each licensee was reportedly investigated, "particularly as to his character and reputation in the community in which he resides."

Licensees included cigar stores, roadside stands, ice cream shoppes, filling stations, etc., etc., as well as taverns, restaurants, and grocery stores.

The Bangor Egg Company, in Bangor, got into the act as a distributor. And in Houlton the Army & Navy Store – on Main Street, next to Newberry's – advertised that it had added beer to its more traditional lineup of outdoor wear and camping gear. As important, beer – thousands and thousands of cases of it – poured into Maine. By land and by sea it came. There were bottles and kegs galore... from breweries throughout New York and New Jersey and the rest of New England and Milwaukee and St. Louis, too. The *Portland Press Herald* reported that there were over 1,150,000 bottles standing by as of June 30th. "Rumble and gurgle" is the term used by the *Bangor Daily News* to describe the mountains of brew arriving from near and far. The *Lewiston Evening Journal* simply said of all the beer: "It'll Be Here In Oceans."

The Day

Louise Hall, now 85 and living in Portland, was 22 then and living in her home town of Camden. She recalls July 1st vividly (even though she and her family weren't beer drinkers): "It was a big day. Everyone was awful happy. They were rejoicing. Especially the menfolk." Adds Louise: "There were an awful lot of people who missed it (beer)."

Across the state in Rumford, however, there appears to have been less rejoicing. Stuart Martin, 88 and a lifelong resident of the area, puts it this way: "I don't think it was euphoria or anything. That's because people had been drinking it (beer... either home brew or smuggled in from Canada) anyway."

cont'd. on page 80

Ad, *Bangor Daily News*, June 13, 1933. If any Maine farmers did heed the advice of this ad and did plant barley it is certainly hoped that it was of the slow-yield variety: it would be 53 years before a Maine brewer – David Geary, in 1986 – arrived on the scene.

Ad, 1933. Hittleman Goldenrod was one of many ready-to-roll-again breweries that emphasized old-time flavor in its advertising.

... *Taste* THAT SATISFIES EVEN "THE MAN WHO REMEMBERS"

THERE is superior taste in GOLD-ENROD. There is a full-bodied creaminess, a deliciousness, a tang and zip that will satisfy even "the man who remembers."

To achieve this taste, only the finest ingredients obtainable anywhere in the world are accepted for GOLDENROD. These are treated according to a brewing formula absolutely unique — and by brewing methods that combine the best of the old with the best of the new in technical improvement.

GOLDENROD is always fully aged and full legal strength.

We'd like you to try GOLDENROD. We think it has such a fine and distinctive flavor that, even blindfolded, you'll be able to distinguish it from other beers. You'll join the millions of GOLDENROD fans who are saying— *"that's* GOLDENROD—it tastes better!"

Sold on draught and by the bottle at good restaurants, hotels and stores everywhere. Get some today!

"Since 1873"

GOLDENROD
Certified LAGER BEER

Hittleman Goldenrod Brewery, Inc., Brooklyn, N.Y.

Goldenrod's Bangor-area distributor, the Bangor Egg Company, obviously had a problem with the word "lager." They misspelled it – as "larger" – not only in their July 1st ads in the *Bangor Daily News* but in those that ran July 2nd and 3rd as well. But "lager" or "larger," people were glad to see it back..

"Goldenrod Is Coming"

In the days before THE DAY - July 1st, 1933 - numerous brewers began their campaign to capture the Maine market. Some of the brands that lined up in the race for the golden amber gold included Kings Beer ("The Beer Your Grandfather Drank"), Trommer's ("The Beer That Brings Back Old Time Memories"), Blatz ("Famous Milwaukee Brewed Beer"), Aetna Special Dinner Ale ("That Creamy Satisfying Beverage"), Paramount ("Try the Famous Beer of Brooklyn"), Elizabeth Brew ("Brewed And Aged As In The Good Old Days"), Rheingold ("You'll Like the Mellow Taste"), and Pickwick Ale ("Delicious Flavor/Highest Quality").

The brewery that certainly seemed the most determined to make its mark in Maine, though, was the Hittleman Goldenrod Brewery of Brooklyn. With roots that stretched back to the 1860s, the brewery decided to concentrate less on the New York market and more on New England. A sales office was established in Boston. The brewery sponsored an every-Friday-night radio broadcast – dubbed the *Goldenrod Revue* – from the Hub. Reported the October 1933 issue of *Brewery Management & Engineering*, a beer industry trade magazine: "The Hittleman Goldenrod Brewery, Inc. is devoting major efforts to selling its beer throughout New England, particularly Massachusetts, and is cutting a wide swath in brewery marketing in this territory." The "wide swath" definitely included Maine. Beginning with a series of "Goldenrod Is Coming!" teaser ads in late June, the Brooklyn brewer pretty much saturated Maine's newspapers with ads. And it wasn't the least bit modest, either. Slogans and superlatives used to ballyhoo Goldenrod included: "The thrill you've been waiting for!" / "The Beer That Took New England By Storm" / "All New England's Talking!" / "America's Choice" / "The beer with the Taste that has thrilled the Nation!" It paid off... for awhile, any-

way. An article in the July 4th *Kennebec Journal* stated that over 30,000 cases and hundreds of kegs of Goldenrod had already been "transported from the Maine State Pier to Bath, Bangor, Biddeford, Augusta, Lewiston and Waterville for local delivery." The *KJ* also reported that the trucks used for delivery, "heralding the approach of an old-fashioned glass of Goldenrod lager," were festooned with banners and flying streamers. Go, Goldenrod!

All the effort eventually proved to be for naught: Goldenrod as a brand ceased to exist in 1946; the brewing company that brewed it ceased to exist in 1951.

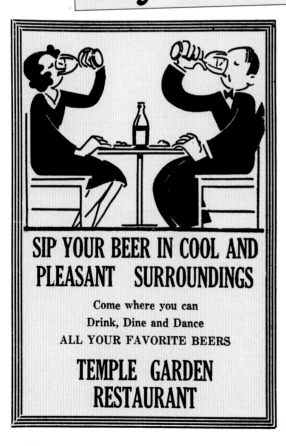

SIP YOUR BEER IN COOL AND
PLEASANT SURROUNDINGS

Come where you can
Drink, Dine and Dance
ALL YOUR FAVORITE BEERS

TEMPLE GARDEN
RESTAURANT

The *Portland Press Herald* certainly had the most dramatic headline on Back-To-Beer Day. But the *Waterville Morning Sentinel* wasn't far behind. And I think it had the most beguiling ads. Reproduced here are two that I especially liked.

THE BEST BEER
& THE BEST FOOD = **Good Cheer**

And You'll Find Good Cheer at Gabby's!

Make Your Selection From Over
Ten Different Brews

SILVER STREET VARIETY STORE

15 SILVER STREET   TELEPHONE 395

"Rivers, Lakes, Aye, Oceans Of Beer"

There were beer advertisements galore in almost every newspaper in the state when beer came marching home. The July 1st edition of the *Waterville Morning Sentinel* led the way with a resounding 36 beer-related ads, while the *Portland Press Herald* sported 29 and both the *Lewiston Daily Sun* and the *Bangor Daily News* chimed in with 23. The rush and crush of getting the ads in on time led, understandably, to quite a few misspellings. Rheingold, then a well-known Brooklyn, New York brand, came out both "Rhinegold" (two times, in fact, both in the *Kennebec*

Journal) and "Reingold" (again in the *KJ*). Old Homestead, a soon-to-be-forgotten brand from Boston, ended up as "Old Homstead" (*Bangor Daily News*); New York's famous Jacob Ruppert's became "Jacob Rupert's" (*Rockland Courier-Gazette*); and Molson turned up as "Malsom" (*Portland Press Herald*). My favorite, though, was the Model Food Store's ad in the *Sanford Tribune And Advocate*: the Model managed to convert Utica Club into "Uticah Club."

"Anywhere – Anytime"

Of the well over 150 beer-related ads – misspelled words and all – placed in Maine newspapers in late June and early July of 1933 this has to be the most intriguing. Even mysterious. It

appeared in the July 1st and July 5th issues of *The Bath Daily Times*. It then disappeared.

The newspapers of the day portrayed varying degrees of excitement as well. The *Portland Press Herald* sported a front page/full eight columns headline that read: "Rivers, Lakes, Aye, Oceans Of Beer, Flow In Maine." Great stuff! The *Waterville Morning Sentinel's* headline, also front page/full eight-columns, was certainly spirited, too. It read: "City Swims In New 3.2 Beer." Beer's return didn't rate a full eight columns in the *Biddeford Daily Journal*, but a front-page subhead announced that "King Beer Given Circus Welcome Here As Trucks Roll." In Lewiston it was the wonderfully alliterative "Foamy Fluid Flowing Freely" in the *Daily Sun*. The *Rockland Courier-Gazette* came up with a phrase that wasn't a headline but that should have been: "Beer! Magic Beer!" The paper then went on to comment "It (beer) is on everybody's lips today, and on a good many lips (there is) some of the three point two itself". Other papers were decidedly more ho hum. The ho hummest of all was probably the *Presque Isle Star Herald*, which carried a short write-up entitled "Beer Now On Sale in Presque Isle."

Regardless of the degree of rejoicing, though, there was no denying that the business in beer was good on the day of its return. The *Sanford Tribune And Advocate* reported that about 30 grocery and drug stores were selling beer and were "doing a rushing business." From the (Caribou) *Aroostook Republican*: "Wholesalers were put to it to keep the demand supplied." The *Houlton Pioneer Times*, too, described both take-out and over-the-counter business as "rushing," while "brisk" was the word used by *The Bath Daily Times*. "Beer was the order of the day in every restaurant" ventured the *Bangor Daily News*, adding "Good healthy business was reported by nearly every establishment carrying the new beverage and not a few of these sold out their first supply long before midnight and had to put in extra orders." (Playing at the Park Theatre in Bangor, not coincidentally, was a movie entitled *What! No Beer?*. Starring Buster Keaton as a taxidermist and Jimmy Durante as a barber, it told of the pair's adventures – and misadventures – in running a brewery.). The (Portland) *Sunday Telegram* declared that "thousands of bottles (of beer) were drained and taps were seldom shut." And in Biddeford, where the foamy beverage was being sold for 10¢ a glass, the *Daily Journal* commented that "Biddeford appeared to be sharing quite a little in the employment that has been created by the brew." (The *Daily Journal* also carried an accompanying heartwarming story. Bylined Presque Isle, its headline was "Beer Sends Potato Prices Up" and the text explained that Aroostook County was experiencing a sharp increase in the value of its spuds because the return of beer translated to a sharp increase in the demand for potato chips. "Aroostook has been hard hit by the depression, but the new beer may be a business life-saver," closed out the article.).

So business was good – if not carnival-like – on July 1st, 1933. Augusta Police Chief John J. O'Connell appeared to sum it all up best when he remarked, "People seem happy to have beer again and to use it in the proper manner."

Bunker Hill And Old Musty, Too

I've always thought of the model in this glorious 1898 lithograph as "The Woman in White." A.G. Van Nostrand's Bunker Hill Breweries, located in Charlestown, Massachusetts, had a history that stretched back to 1821 and that lasted until 1918. And for a hefty chunk of all those years Van Nostrand's two breweries - one for ale; one for lager - quenched many a Mainer's thirst. The favorite? Most likely it was the brewery's fabled PB ("Purest and Best") Ale. But, then again, there was Bunker Hill Lager, Boston Club Lager, and Old Musty Ale, too. The choice was yours.

Lithographed poster, 1898

Circa 1900
lithographed
poster

The "King Of Portsmouth"

If ever there had been a king of Portsmouth, New Hampshire... that king would have been Frank Jones (1832-1902). Among his achievements: two-term Portsmouth mayor; two-term New Hampshire congressman; almost New Hampshire governor (he lost by a scant 2,000 votes in 1880); president of the Boston and Maine Railroad, the Granite State Fire Insurance Company, several other corporations. His foremost claim to fame, though, was his brewery, "modestly" named the Frank Jones Brewing Company. He boasted that it was "The Largest Ale Brewery in the World" and he was probably about right. He was so big he even operated a branch, from 1889 to 1903, in Boston. This lithograph dates from those years. It is probably from 1900 or so.

A fair percentage of Frank's output ended up in Maine, where it was distributed for many years by a man named Moses Morrill. Moses operated a depot (distribution point) on Fore Street in Portland and through it flowed, literally, untold kegs of Jones' Imperial XXX Golden Sparkling Champagne Ale, as well as Jones' pale and amber ales.

COMPLIMENTS OF
FRANK · JONES · BREWING · CO.
LIMITED
PORTSMOUTH, N. H.   BOSTON, MASS.

"The Finest Temperance Drinks In New England"

The Ingalls brothers, Robert and Hiram, played both sides of Maine's alcohol vs. no alcohol tempest. Either individually or together they manufactured beer in Portland from 1864 until 1880 or so. But they also manufactured a full line of soda and "soft" (i.e., containing little or no alcohol) beers. And by the 1890s they could – and did – boast of "The Finest Temperance Drinks in New England."

Courtesy of Rick Poore, Standish

Circa 1895 Ingalls Brothers' trade advertising cards

Circa 1933 advertising sign

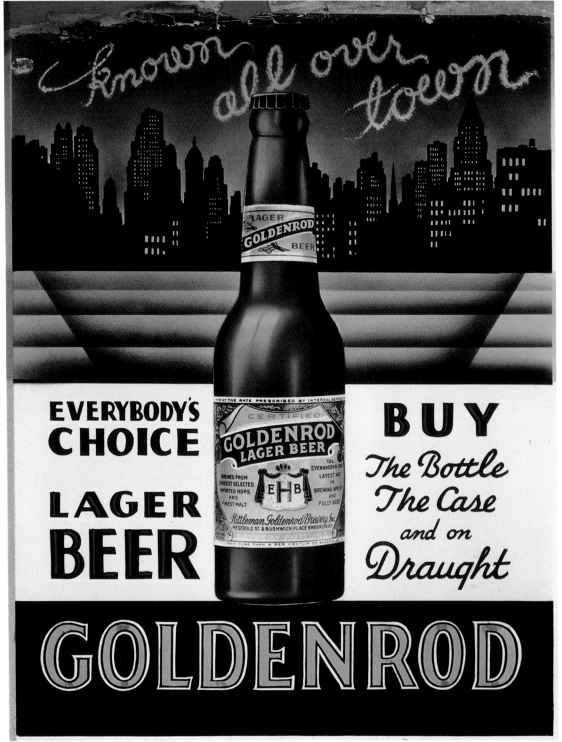

Goldenrod

When beer - legally - came back to Maine in the summer of 1933 Goldenrod was there. As a featured player. Sure, there were many other brands, too. But it was the Hittleman Goldenrod Brewing Company, of Brooklyn, brewers of Goldenrod, that created the most presence. And spent the most advertising bucks. For weeks before the grand Beer-Is-Back Day of July 1st there were "Goldenrod is coming!" teaser ads in newspapers throughout the state. These were followed by a burst of "Goldenrod is here!" ads. Nor was the brewery bashful in its claims. Slogans and superlatives used to herald Goldenrod included: "The Beer That Took New England By Storm," "All New England's Talking," "America's Choice," "The beer with the taste that has thrilled the Nation!," and "The thrill you've been waiting for!" Alas, however, it was pretty much all for naught. Hittleman Goldenrod was soon buried under the marketing avalanche of far bigger brewers.

Circa 1933 advertising tray

Circa 1933
matchbook cover

"All the Favorite Brands"

On July 1, 1933 - the day of beer's triumphant return to Maine - the *Waterville Morning Sentinel*'s headline was "City Swims In New 3.2 Beer"… and there were no less than 33 ads for places proudly proclaiming that, yes, they were serving the golden nectar. The Exchange Hotel, located on Front Street near the Common, was one of the more prominent proclaimers. A large ad boasted "All the Favorite Brands of Boston and New York on Draught or in Bottles." Featured were King's ("The Beer Your Grandfather Drank"), Pickwick Ale ("Delicious Flavor" / "Highest Quality"), Rheingold ("Guaranteed by many state chemists to be the finest product on the market"), Pabst Blue Ribbon ("Milwaukee's Finest"), and, of course, Goldenrod ("At last - the thrill you've been waiting for!").

Ox Head In Cans

The beer can was introduced to the world in 1935. Invented by the American Can Company, it was first utilized by the G. Krueger Brewing Company, of Newark, New Jersey. Many thought it would prove a bust. But it didn't. Soon most of America's brewers were packaging their beer and ale in cans, too. Early canned entries in the Maine market included Ballantine, Schlitz, Pabst, Old Tap Select (from the Enterprise Brewing Company, of Fall River, Massachusetts)… and Ox Head and Mule Head, both products of the Wehle Brewing Company, of West Haven, Connecticut.

Circa 1935 point-of-purchase display sign

The Glory Of Color

Breweries and breweriana – beer advertising and packaging – can be beautiful. And colorful. Over this and the next eight pages is a veritable Maine Micro-Brewery Colorama. Enjoy.

Label, Allagash Brewing Co., Portland

When I asked Allagash proprietor Rob Tod about his distinctive label design here's what he had to say: "I wanted to conjure up an image of a pristine place where people want to be." Rob also made it clear that, to him, this pristine place is in good old New England. "I used," he said, "a lot of fall colors and gave it a woodcut look: I wanted a real New England feel to it."

Keg Label, *Andrew's Brewing Co., Lincolnville*

The faithful pooch pictured here is modeled after Andrew's Brewing Company prexy Andy Hazen's golden retriever, Boomer. ("Actually it's modeled more after Boomer's great uncle, Miller... but," laughs Andy, "it somehow didn't seem right for the model for our beer to be named 'Miller'.") At present Boomer/Miller is used only for keg labels, but Andy hopes to eventually move into bottles and to use the design for their labels as well.

T-Shirt Design, *Atlantic Brewing Co., Bar Harbor*

If this isn't the most attractive T-shirt design in the entire country it must be pretty darned close! The slogan, dreamed up by Atlantic proprietor Doug Maffucci's sister-in-law Tammie, was, explains Doug, "just a play on the 'Save The Whales' campaign. But," he adds, "it was apropos because at the time (c. 1989) the American beer market was short on hearty ales."

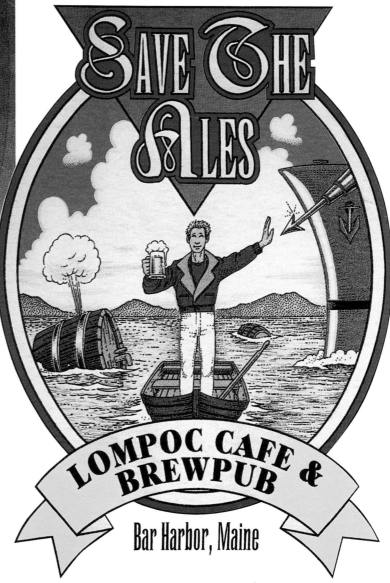

Label Design, Bar Harbor Brewing Co., Bar Harbor

I love the color orange... so this label design is a favorite of mine. The thirst-provoking mug was the work of Mohr Signs, of Bar Harbor, while the remainder of the artwork was designed by Downeast Graphics, of Ellsworth... all, of course, with input from Bar Harbor Brewing's proprietors, Suzi and Tod Foster.

Photo, October 1995, Bear Brewpub, Orono

Opened in September 1995, the Bear Brewpub is the creation of Yugoslav-native Milos Blagojevic. This is the sign – above the brewpub's entrance – that beckons to the thirsty and/or the hungry.

Photo, March 1996, Bray's Brewpub & Eatery, Naples

When co-proprietor Michele Windsor first laid eyes upon photographs of the buildings that were to become Bray's Brewpub she exclaimed "Wow! This is beautiful." It's easy to see why.
P.S. That's the brewhouse in the smaller building, back left; the brewpub and restaurant in the bigger building, front right.

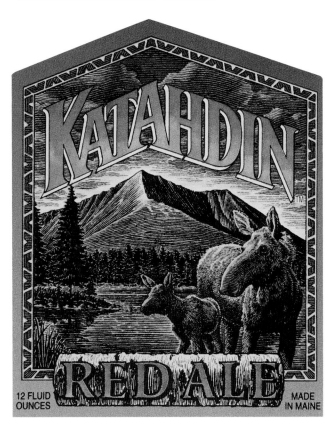

Label, Casco Bay Brewing Company, Portland

Of Casco Bay's three "regulars" – Katahdin Red Ale, Katahdin Golden Beer, and Katahdin Stout – it's the Red that is the most popular. When I asked brewery founder Mike LaCharite which of the three was his personal favorite, he just smiled and answered "I like them all."

Label Element, Geary's Hampshire Special Ale, D.L. Geary Brewing Co., Portland

Created by Portland graphic arts designer Peter Stock, this is the scene that graces Geary's Hampshire Special Ale label. The only problem: when the label is on the bottle you almost need a magnifying glass to see the scene. That, however, is the idea. Admits Geary founder and president David Geary: "It draws people in. They pick up the bottle to get a closer look. It's" he adds, "more like a fine wine label than a beer label." Hampshire Special – a fuller-bodied brew than its cousin, Geary's Pale – is available only from November to March, the time of year, says David, "when we need a little extra fuel in the tank."

Photo, August 1995, Great Falls Brewing Co., Auburn

The Great Falls Brewing Company – named after the nearby great falls of the Androscoggin – makes its home on the first floor of the quite magnificent circa 1880 Goff Block in downtown Auburn.

Photo, August 1995. Neon Sign, Gritty McDuff's, Portland

Was he a Charles Dickens' character? Was he a turn-of-the-century prizefighter? Was he an infamous scoundrel? Just who was this guy named Gritty? To find out turn to page 138.

Photo, October 1995, Gritty McDuff's, Freeport

This is the sign that greets people as they arrive at Gritty's/Freeport. It's an enlargement of the brewery's Best Bitter logo... and features none other than Ed Stebbins, Gritty's congenial brewmaster, pint of ale in hand. "That's Ed in his younger and better-looking days," chuckles Gritty's president Richard Pfeffer.

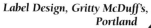

Label Design, Gritty McDuff's, Portland

When I asked Gritty co-proprietor Richard Pfeffer "Why Black Fly?," he laughed. "We wanted a good Maine-type word to describe our black beer," said he, continuing "and what better than the "Maine State Bird?"

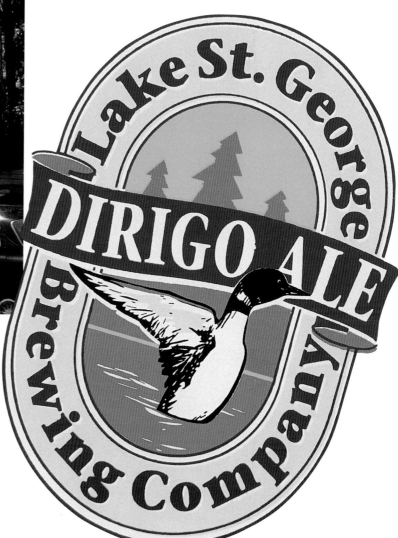

Photo, August 1995, Kennebunkport Brewing Co./Federal Jack's Brew Pub, Kennebunk

Federal Jack's, Kennebunkport Brewing Company's brewpub, takes its name from a schooner built in Kennebunkport harbor in the early 1800s. "I thought it was a neat name," explains brewery founder Fred Forsley, "and it tied everything – then and now – together because it was built here on the banks of the harbor."

Keg Label, Lake St. George Brewing Company, Liberty

If you were to visit Lake St. George co-proprietor Dan McGovern's house and brewery you'd understand why he and partner Kellon Thames named their endeavor what they did: the view of the lake from the house/brewery is, quite simply, spectacular. And the loon on the label? "Well, we sat down and asked ourselves," says Dan, "what do you think of when you think of Lake St. George?" The answer, for Dan and Kellon at least, is loons. "There are," Dan assured me, "lots of loons out there."

Labels, Sea Dog Brewing Co., Bangor and Camden

"Sea Dog' is my dog's nickname," Sea Dog founding father and president Pete Camplin, Sr. is proud to tell. Especially as his dog – real name: Barney – is a Great Pyrenees, a breed generally not known for its love of the ocean. Barney, however, loves the water. "He's been going sailing with me since he was a puppy," Pete again says with pride. The likeness of Barney shown here really is just that... a likeness. It's from an actual photo. The hat, admits Pete, was added.

Photo, November 1995, Maine Coast Brewing Co., Bar Harbor

Cheers! Left to right, Joe Kerber, Mary Rademacher, Paul Rademacher, and Dick Antholzner, all from the Buffalo, New York area, enjoying themselves outside Maine Coast on a warm autumn afternoon.

Photo, September 1995, Shipyard Brewing Co., Portland

The huge – it's 20' x 24' – mural that adorns Shipyard's brewery is based on Shipyard's Export Ale label. The label, in turn, is based on a painting by Kennebunk artist Ken Hendricksen. And the painting, again in turn, is based on a photo – of a ship making its way through Kennebunkport Harbor in the early 1800s – that Ken discovered in the Brick Store Museum in Kennebunk. The result is worth all the effort. The mural is quite a splendid sight.

Label Design, Shipyard Brewing Co., Portland

You have to like this label design. *Beverage World* magazine liked it, too: it awarded the label's designer – Chris Hadden of Chris Hadden Design, in Portland – its Beverage Packaging Award for 1995. "Basically," Chris told me, "we were just sitting around brainstorming and we decided we wanted a moose who was whimsical looking." Well, whimsical he is. Alas, however, he's also endangered. When I spoke with Shipyard head Fred Forsley in March 1996 he told me that "A friendly brewer from the north has concerns about the use of the moose." Added Fred: "So we have voluntarily decided to rename our brown ale." A contest to come up with a new name is in the offing.

Photo, March 1996, Stone Coast Brewing Co., Portland

Constructed in 1885 by the Portland Packing Company, the building that is now home to Stone Coast Brewing is reminiscent of many of the pre-prohibition breweries that once dotted America: it's big and it's brick and it's quite beauteous.

Photo, November 1995, Sugarloaf Brewing Co./Theo's Brewpub, Carrabasset Valley

Sugarloaf Brewing takes its name, quite naturally, from adjoining Sugarloaf/USA, while Theo's honors skiing visionary Theodore A. Johnsen.

Coaster, Sunday River Brewing Co., Bethel

Yes, coasters (also called beer pads) can be beautiful. This is my favorite Maine coaster. The name "Black Bear" came about, not surprisingly, in honor of the University of Maine black bear. "He looks more like a dog, though, to be honest," states Sunday River founder Grant Wilson. "He's very serene, just standing there."

"The Amber Fluid Comes Back To Bangor With A Bang" read the suggested headline for this Wide World wire service photo. Dated July 4, 1933, it purported to show the joy in the Lumber City the day beer actually came back, July 1st. Other than including the fact that Bangor was in Maine, however, the accompanying write-up gave little worthwhile – such as the name of the gleeful establishment in which the photo was taken – information. So, 63 years and one month later, in August 1995, my wife Catherine and I drove up to Bangor and spent a very full day playing sleuth.

We researched in the Bangor Public Library, in the Bangor Historical Society, and at the *Bangor Daily News*, and we talked with innumerable oldtimers – in retirement homes, in bars, and on the street – only to come away with nothing concrete. There was a consensus, though, and it was that the photo – and it's a wonderful photo – was snapped at Ye Brass Rail. It makes sense: located at 202 Exchange Street, Ye Brass Rail was Bangor's pace-setter in terms of "Beer Is Back!" advertising that notable June/July; featured four brews on draught and five more by the bottle (at 20 cents a bottle); boasted of "the largest and finest beer cooling machine in the state;" and promised to serve one and all beer that was "Rich, Creamy and Cool."

It sounds like a good place to have been that July 1, 1933.

Courtesy of the National Archives, Washington, D.C.

Beyond 1933

Not an awful lot of tremendous importance happened in the world of beer for the next 40 years or so. At least four Maine firms, in 1933, did apply for a license to brew. The four were: the Eagle Beverage & Products Co., of Rumford; the Eldridge Brewing Co., Inc., of Kittery; Beverage Distributors, Inc., of Portland; and Eastern Distributors, Inc., of Lewiston. But none of them ever did brew.

Noteworthy was the *Beer Barrel Polka*, first recorded in Czechoslovakia in 1934. Originally entitled *Skoda Lasky (Lost Love)*, it was eventually recorded by a host of American artists, including Kay Kyser, Barry Wood, and the act that made it a smash hit, the Andrews Sisters. Regardless of who sang it few could resist the magic of the lyrics:

> "Roll out the barrel,
> We'll have a barrel of fun;
> Roll out the barrel,
> We've got the blues on the run."

Sheet music cover, 1939. Born James King Kern Kyser in North Carolina in 1906, Kay Kyser was a big band leader par excellence from 1933 on. His nationally broadcast radio show, *Kay Kyser's Kollege of Musical Knowledge*, premiered in 1938. He recorded his version of the *Beer Barrel Polka* a year later, in 1939.

Then there was the birth – for better or worse – of the beer can. It's been over 60 years since the G. (for Gottfried) Krueger Brewing Company, of Newark, New Jersey, introduced canned beer to the world in January of 1935. Actually, they didn't introduce it to the world... just to the prospective beerbuyers of Richmond, Virginia. The reason for Richmond was simple: Krueger management was fearful the can might flop, so they selected a test market on the fringe of their sales area, far, far away from the bulk of their business in the Newark/New York City area.

HE'S BEEN THAT WAY SINCE THEY STARTED PUTTING BEER IN CANS!

Comic post card, circa 1936

Photo, Richmond, Virginia, early 1935. As part of its Richmond launch, Krueger sent a package containing four sample tin cans into a thousand Richmond homes in the spring of 1934. Included in each sample package was a questionnaire that allowed each family to give their views on canned beer in general and the four cans specifically. The result, in the winter/spring of 1935, was a finely-tuned campaign for Krueger in cans.

But the beer can - actually developed by the American Can Company - did not flop. Quite to the contrary, it proved to be a smash success. While many people obviously gave it a try for novelty's sake, many came to appreciate the fact that the can was lighter in weight than a bottle, and was more compact, too. They became repeat Krueger-in-the-can customers.

Krueger's success, naturally, was soon common knowledge throughout the brewing community. Before long most every other American brewer was canning at least some of its output, too. First to arrive in Maine was P. Ballantine & Sons, also of Newark. Their copper-colored Keglined (the trademark name of American Can) cans arrived in October of 1935. Other early entries were Mule Head Ale and Beer from the Wehle Brewing Company of West Haven, Connecticut; Old Tap Select Stock Ale and Export Lager Beer, from the Enterprise Brewing Company of Fall River, Massachusetts; and a pair of then Milwaukee giants, Pabst and Schlitz. Schlitz's can, incidentally, held its just-developed Vitamin D Beer. It was hailed by the brewery as "one of the greatest brewing achievements of all time." Maybe so, but the Auto City Brewing Company, of Detroit, went one step further in early 1937: it added vitamin G (riboflavin) as well as vitamin D to its Altweiser Beer. All this wholesomeness came to a halt, however, in early 1940 when the Federal Alcoholic Adminisration ruled that beer labeling could not make mention of any vitamins the beer might contain. The FAA's reasoning: such labeling might cause some people to believe that beer had curative powers.

World War II had several effects on beer and the brewing industry. For starters, it became patriotic to consume beer by the quart rather than by the 12-ounce bottle. (Cans became almost nonexistent on the home front for the duration.). This was due to the nation's acute metal shortage... and the indisputable fact that a cap went further on the larger-sized bottle. So 32-ounce bottles became "Victory Quarts" and brewers exhorted the beerdrinking public to "Do Your Part - Buy The Quart," "Save Caps To Beat The Japs" and "Help To Win - Save The Tin." (Drinking draught beer, of course, was even more patriotic: there were *no* caps involved!).

The big beer news from WWII, though, was bad. Tin was far from the only item in short supply. Rubber, meat, butter, and many other commodities were hard to come by as well. So, too, was barley, causing many brewers to cut the barley they could get with more-plentiful corn or rice. The result: lighter, less robust brew. Legend has it, moreover, that even this lighter beer wasn't light enough for most of the nation's newest contingent of beerdrinkers... the Rosie the Riveteers of America. Whereas women, before the war, bought beer for the household, during the war they started buying it for themselves. They were doing "men's work," they reasoned, so why shouldn't they drink beer the way men did, too? But the ladies liked it light, real light, often going so far as to thin their beer with water. Brewers, elated at the prospect of finally being able to break big into the female market, obliged... and, in effect, thinned the beer right at the brewery. Less bitterness was also the order of

Beer ads from 1942, the year the War Production Board began the rationing of bottle caps... and America had Victory Quarts as well as Victory Gardens.

the day, so less and less hops - which gives beer its characteristic taste - were blended in. Schlitz, then an industry giant, went so far as to adopt "Just The Kiss Of The Hops" as its slogan.

After the war the trend to lighter and lighter - translate blander and blander - continued. And those that brewed blandness the best seemed to be the big boys. Anheuser-Busch. Schlitz. Pabst. Etc. You know who they are. Blandness and bigness appeared to go hand in hand, with the result that the number of operating breweries across the land dropped alarmingly, from approximately 750 in 1934 to but 82 in 1980. And many of those 82 were branch plants (A-B, for example, was operating ten plants in 1980.).

Things looked dim.

Before we see, however, how this sad story became a glad story, let us take a look at ale: what it is; some ale yarns (ale tales, if you will); why Mainers have been partial to it; and how it helped lead the way back in the anti-bland attack.

Hail, Hail Ale

In WINTER'S TALE, Shakespeare wrote "A quart of ale is a dish fit for a king." And Shakespeare knew what-of he spoke: his father was an ale conner, an official taster of ale who had the authority to condemn a bad batch or order it to be sold at a lower price if it were not up to snuff.

Ale is more or less *the* drink of the British Isles. (The word "bridal," in fact, comes from the words "bride ale," the name given to a special

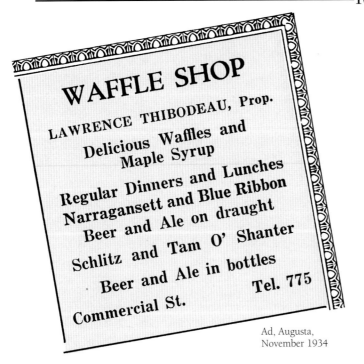

Ad, Augusta,
November 1934

Ad, Bangor, March 1935. Notice the misspelling of "Ballantine."

Ad, Waterville, April 1935. The Harvard Brewing Company
was located in Lowell, Mass.

Ad, Camden, circa 1936

ale brewed to honor the bride and the wedding feast in English days of yore.). It differs from its close relative, lager, in several respects. It has a much shorter aging period. It has a more pronounced hop flavor and is generally more full-bodied. It's a brew you want to chew. Porter and stout are both types of ale.

America has certainly had its ale tradition, too. Samuel Adams, Israel Putnam (a hero of the Battle of Bunker Hill), and Thomas Chitenden (the first governor of Vermont) all did some commercial brewing of ale. And the Father of our Country, George Washington, loved his porter. To this day there's a recipe for it - written out in his own handwriting - in the collection of the New York Public Library.

Of special note is Matthew Vassar. The man who founded America's first privately endowed college for women (in 1861) made his fortune as a Poughkeepsie, New York ale brewer. He was, in fact, such a devoted ale man that he steadfastly refused to switch even a portion of his production to lager, in spite of its growing popularity

cont'd. on page 108

Ale For Sale

Over the next seven pages is a graphic tribute to ale and its longtime popularity and staying power in Maine. Breweries, bars, grocery stores, restaurants: they all had ale for sale. And they still do.

Dawson's was a product of Dawson's Brewery, Inc., which was located in New Bedford, Massachusetts and which operated until 1977. Its longtime slogan was "Time Out For Dawson's!" and it, in the 1930s, was the first brewery to sponsor the Red Sox on radio. Only two others have in all the years since. Can you name the two? Answer below.

Answer: Narragansett ("Hi, Neighbor, Have A 'Gansett") and Anheuser-Busch.

Ad, Portland, May 1937

Frank Jones was undoubtedly the most famous name in northern New England brewing history. Frank Jones, the man, was born in Barrington, New Hampshire in 1832, moved to Portsmouth at age 16, and there left his mark as two-term mayor, two-term congressman, president of the Boston & Maine Railroad, proprietor of the Rockingham and the colossal Wentworth-by-the Sea hotels, and an-almost governor: he missed being elected in 1880 by a mere 2,000 votes.

But it was in brewing that Frank really made his mark: formed in 1859, the Frank Jones Brewing Company was headquartered in Portsmouth with a very sizable branch brewery in Boston, and was so successful that by the turn-of-the-century Frank could proclaim that he was the "Largest Ale Brewer In The World."

Frank Jones Ale survived in one form or another through 1955. In recent years the name has enjoyed a rebirth as part of the micro boom.

The Albany/Troy area of New York was long noted for its ales. Scottish immigrant Peter Ballantine – as in Ballantine Ale – got his brewing start in Troy in the late 1820s. There was an Anderson's Ale (what a great name!) brewed in Albany from 1862 to 1872. And there was the Fitzgerald Brothers Brewing Company, of Troy, brewer of Gerryowen Ale and Fitzgerald Ale and Porter – among other products – from 1866 to 1962.

Ad, Portland, Feb. 1947

CLOSE COVER FOR SAFETY

Pooler's Lunch

"The Draft-Rite System"

Cooled by
Frigidaire Flowing
Cold System
MAIN STREET
FAIRFIELD, MAINE

Our Ales on Tap Kept
at proper pressure With

Ladies Invited

SHORT ON SAILS

CLOSE COVER BEFORE STRIKING

AIRPORT LUNCH

Beer and Ale On
Draught
Lobsters and Light Lunches
1335 CONGRESS STREET
PORTLAND, MAINE

MERTON L. CARVER
Proprietor

a
can go
8 days
without
a drink

—Who the

wants to be
a camel

—?

Matchbook covers,
Portland and Fairfield,
circa 1955

—107—

Ad, Dover- Foxcroft, July 1968

Ad, Dexter, July 1968

Ad, Houlton, December 1968

after being introduced to America in 1840. It was not a smooth move: his brewery failed in 1896. Matthew's fame lives on, however, in a little ditty that Vassar students are yet known to sing:

> As so you see, for old V.C.
> Our love shall never fail.
> Full well we know
> That all we owe
> To Matthew Vassar's ale!

Another little ditty, entitled *"Some Lines On Ale,"* was penned in the Washington Tavern in Lowell, Massachusetts in 1848 by none other than Edgar Allan Poe. Here's how it goes:

> Fill with mingled cream and amber
> I will drain that glass again.
> Such hilarious visions clamber
> Through the chamber of my brain –
> Quaintest thoughts – queerest fancies
> Come to life and fade away.
> What care I how time advances?
> I am drinking ale today.

Of perhaps greater significance is that people from east of the Hudson – and that certainly includes Mainers – have always had a noticable leaning toward ale. Maybe it's because ale's hearty character fits our character. Maybe it's because we have more respect for our good old English heritage. Maybe it's because we like to be a little different – a little more distinctive, if you will – than the rest of those states out there. Or maybe it's a combination of all of the above. Who knows? What is known is that, when all seemed lost in the blandness = bigness/bigness = blandness parade, it was micro-brewed ale that led the way back to taste. And Maine was – and is – a major contributor to that taste. Hail, hail ale.

Comic postcard, circa 1955

Even in New England's darkest brewing hours - before the charge
of the micro-brewery brigade - there was always ale - of one sort
or another - to provide a burst of taste and a ray of hope.

Part III ≠ New Brewers

They started it all: Maine brewing vanguards Alan Pugsley, Karen Geary, and David Geary line up outside the then-fledgling D.L. Geary Brewing Company, Portland, March 1988.

A man named Jack McAuliffe is generally credited with being the father of the micro-brewing movement in America. McAuliffe was a U.S. sailor stationed in Scotland in the mid-1970s. All around him there flowed hearty and robust Scottish ales. Jack loved them. His problem was his military pay: it failed to allow him to partake of as many brews as he might have liked. The solution: to simulate those brews via homebrewing. The results weren't bad. Jack kept on homebrewing. And when his service days were over and he returned to the States he kept on homebrewing, too. After a while he decided to share his achievements with others. The result was the formation, with partners Suzy Stern and Jane Zimmerman, of the New Albion Brewing Company in Sonoma, California in 1977. Jack's brewery, mostly because of undercapitalization, eventually failed. He ceased operations in 1983. But Jack McAuliffe had planted the seed that small can be beautiful. And once that seed started to sprout, there was no stopping it.

By the time of New Albion's demise there were brewing juices beginning to ebb and flow in Maine. First, though, came Portland's Three Dollar Dewey's. Opened on the very last day of February 1981, Dewey's was the dream of beer maven Alan Eames. Eames envisioned - and created - a no-frills English-style pub that featured a selection of ales and beers second to none. It was, in many ways, a catalyst for what was to come. "Dewey's educated an entire generation of beer drinkers," wrote beer savant Al Diamon in the June 29, 1995 issue of Portland's *Casco Bay Weekly*, "so that by the time good

Richard Pfeffer, left, and original - and short-term - partners Steve Barnes and Eric Harrison pose outside Maine's first brewpub-to-be, June 1988.

local beer arrived, there'd be someone to drink it." Ed Stebbins, brewmaster at Maine's pioneer brewpub, Gritty McDuff's in Portland, goes one step further. Says Ed: "Gritty's never could have happened without Dewey's. Nobody would have known what we were trying to do."

The state's political wizards chimed in, too. Thanks largely to the efforts of Henry Cabot, they passed *"An Act Concerning the Licensing of Small Maine Breweries"* in the spring of 1985. Henry, called "Harry" by friends, was proprietor of the Pine Cone Public House in Waldoboro. It was his goal to expand it into the Pine Cone Public House and Bakery and Brewpub. It, alas, never happened, but Henry's / Harry's efforts led to legislation that, as defined by Maine's dean of brewers, David Geary, "Created special licensing that permitted small Maine breweries to self-distribute and permitted them to brew and serve on-premises."

Another ingredient in Maine's micro story is the now largely-forgotten Portland Lager. It was the brainchild of Portland residents Jon Bove and Hugh Nazor, who contracted with Hibernia Brewing Company, of Eau Claire, Wisconsin (later with the F.X. Matt Brewing Company, of Utica, New York), to brew a full-bodied beer in early 1986. Buoyed by its sales success, Bove and Nazor talked of opening

their own brewery. They came close, settling on a former textile mill in Lisbon Falls, but saw their dream fade away when the mill burned down in July of 1987. Although never brewed in Maine, Portland Lager did help to further awaken the taste buds of Maine's beer-buying public.

Enter the final ingredients: David and Karen Geary and Alan Pugsley. David is a native of Portland; Karen, of Joliet, Illinois; Alan, of Stratford-on-Avon, England. In 1986 they came together, as told on pages 132-133, to brew Maine's first commercially - and legally! - sold beer since the days when the Babe was on the mound for the Sox. And that's a long, long time ago.

A Decade of Excitement

A lot has happened in the world of Maine brewing since Geary's Pale Ale started satisfying beer drinkers in December 1986. The Maine Brewers' Guild, an organization committed to bettering beer awareness and quality and the responsible consumption of the amber nectar, now boasts a membership that will soon include 25 breweries. They range in size from small and smaller to large and larger. They are scattered from South Berwick and Kennebunk to Bar Harbor and Bangor. Each has a story. Over the next 50 pages, those stories are told.

```
                    STATE OF MAINE

                        ——


              IN THE YEAR OF OUR LORD
          NINETEEN HUNDRED AND EIGHTY-FIVE

                        ——


              S.P. 603 - L.D. 1579

        AN ACT Concerning the Licensing of Small
                  Maine Breweries.
```

Be it enacted by the People of the State of Maine as follows:

   28 MRSA §501, sub-§1-A is enacted to read:

   1-A. Small Maine breweries. Small Maine brew-eries shall pay an annual license fee of .... $50.

For purposes of this section, "small Maine brewery" means a facility that is brewing, lagering and kegging, bottling or packaging its own malt liquors within the State. If an inadequate amount of agri-cultural products used for raw materials exists with-in the State, a holder of a small Maine brewery li-cense may file an affidavit and application with the Bureau of Alcoholic Beverages setting forth the un-availability of raw materials within the State and requesting permission to import those agricultural products from out-of-state. If the bureau finds that there is in fact an inadequate supply of raw materi-als within the State, it may authorize that importa-tion.

A holder of a small Maine brewery license may produce malt liquors containing 25% or less alcohol by volume in an amount not to exceed 50,000 gallons per year, or their metric equivalent.

A holder ·of a small Maine brewery license may sell, on the premises during regular business hours, malt liquors produced at the brewery by the bottle, case or in bulk.

A holder of a small Maine brewery license may sell or deliver his product to licensed retailers and whole-salers. In addition, he may sell, on the premises for consumption off the premises, malt liquors pro-duced at the brewery by the bottle, case or in bulk to licensed retailers, including, but not limited to, retail stores, restaurants and clubs.

A holder of a small Maine brewery license may apply for one license for the sale of liquor for on-premise consumption for a location other than the brewery.

A holder of a small Maine brewery license may list on product labels and in its advertising the list of the ingredients and the product's average percentage of the recommended daily allowances of nutritional re-quirements.

You may well need a magnifying glass to read this... but you will enjoy reading it. It's the Act that legally set micro breweries in motion in Maine. Worthy of special note are the "containing 25% or less alcohol" and "average percentage of the recommended daily allowances of nutritional requirements" phrases.

Exterior, Allagash Brewing Company, October 1995. Rob chose the name "Allagash" because he "thinks people in Maine associate it with a clean and pristine and unspoiled place... a place where they'd like to be."

ALLAGASH BREWING COMPANY
100 INDUSTRIAL WAY, PORTLAND 04103

Rob Tod is a man who knows what he likes. He likes being a brewer.

Born and raised in Concord, Massachusetts, Rob went to college at Middlebury, graduating with a B.A. in 1991. But his major was geology, and because of it he was exposed to more than just a little science. "I spent a lot of time looking down microscopes," the 28-year old states unequivocally. That familiarity with science and lab work was to pay off.

After college Rob spent a couple of years in Colorado, working as a carpenter and handy-

man. How did his parents feel about that, what with his Middlebury degree and all? "They weren't too excited about it," Rob admits. But it, too, was experience that would pay off.

After two years in Colorado, Rob found himself longing for New England. "I missed the people and, believe it or not, the weather," he explains. The result was a return to Vermont, back to Middlebury again. Through a friend he lined up a job at Middlebury's micro, Otter Creek Brewing. It was love from the start. Realizing he'd found his calling, Rob was upfront with the folks at Otter Creek. "I'm going to go off and do this on my own," he told them. And, after exactly a year, that's just what he did. But why did a guy from Massachusetts and Vermont, with a little Colorado tossed in, select Portland, Maine as the site for his venture? Rob fields that one easily: "Portland's at the forefront of having educated consumers, willing to experiment with different types of beer, and of having a wide variety of beers available to consume."

In July of 1994 Rob set up shop in the Turnpike Industrial Park. He admits he had visions of finding an old brick building and transforming it into his dream brewhouse. But practicality won out: at the industrial park he settled into a facility that was problem-free and possessed such mundane - but very necessary - things as water and sewer all hooked up and ready to roll. There being already established brewers, Geary's and Casco Bay, as neighbors was a big plus, too. "We get along," Rob says of his fellow brewers at the Park, and throughout Maine as well. "We realize we're all in the same boat," he explains. Rob shipped his first brew - Allagash White, a Belgian-style wheat beer - in July of 1995. When I interviewed him three months later, in October of 1995, he was all smiles at how things were going. "I'm having a blast," he beamed.

ALLAGASH AT A GLANCE
Sold first beer = 7/95. 1995 production = 123.5 barrels (100% draught; became available in bottles = 5/96). Employees = 2. Major brands = Allagash White, Allagash Double Ale. Available at select locations throughout Maine. For directions and tour/tasting info call (207) 878-5385.

Rob Tod poses for the camera, October 1995. Rob is proud he's put both his college training ("The lab end of brewing is so important,") and his handyman experience ("A small brewer has to be an electrician, a plumber, a carpenter and a welder as well as a brewer.") to good use.

Photo, September 1995. Andrew's Brewing Company occupies part of the Hazen's circa 1795 farmhouse. It's the part where Andy spends the lion's share of his life. "I'm still," he says, "putting in 80-90 hours a week."

ANDREW'S BREWING COMPANY
RFD 1, BOX 4975, LINCOLNVILLE 04849

Maine's unrobust real estate market in the late 1980s turned out to be a blessing for Maine's beer aficionados. That's because it led Andrew "Andy" Hazen to stop making cabinetwork and start making beer.

Andy's a New Englander. But not a Mainer. He was born in Marblehead, Massachusetts in 1945 and grew up there, leaving for "four years of fun and games" with the Air Force, 1963-1967. A civilian once more, Andy attended the University of Colorado, graduating with a B.S. in 1971. Then it was back to Marblehead, where he and his wife Judie, also a Marblehead native, operated a ski shop for three years. But Andy heard the call of Maine. His mother's family was from Lubec, and his father and grandfather jointly owned a summer house in Rangeley. Andy spent a lot of summers in Rangeley.

In 1976 Andy and Judie and their daughter Emily made the move to Maine. To North Anson. "It was my idea," readily admits Andy: "I've always liked the idea of living in the woods." Judie was less enchanted, however, and in 1978 the Hazens departed North Anson for Lincolnville. It was a compromise: Judie wanted the coast (Camden) while Andy still wanted lots of trees. In Lincolnville, Andy continued on with the skill, carpentry, he'd begun in North Anson. He, though, also began to hone a new skill: making beer. "I like beer," Andy laughs, and from 1984 on he created most of what he consumed. "It was better and cheaper," are his words.

Andy's carpentry business sailed along for the better part of a decade. In 1986 the Hazens even built an addition onto their house in order to enlarge the cabinet shop. By the late 1980s, however, business was definitely on the downward trail. The real estate market had gone flat and Andy, who derived much of his income as a subcontractor, went flat with it. By 1989 he and Judie knew something had to give. It was the cabinet business. Turning homebrew into commercial brew increasingly appealed to Andy. "My wife thought I was crazy as a loon," he says. But a visit to Bar Harbor to see Suzi and Tod Foster's operation (please see pages 120-121) helped convince Andy that he really was on the right track. The early 1990s were "market research" years. "Like any homebrewer you develop a lot of friends," he smiles. "People would stop by and I'd press a beer on them and get their opinion." Andy's brews got good reviews. He decided to go for it.

By late 1992 Andrew's Brewing Company was a reality. The cabinet shop had become a brewery. A neighbor bought Andy's very first for-sale beer for a New Year's Day 1993 party. Darby's Restaurant in Belfast became commercial account number one in February. "From there," states Andy, "we just started adding accounts."

Three years and several expansions later, Andy is still adding accounts. He's pleased. But he promptly admits running a small brewery is far from a picnic. "Beer," he says, "is a simple beverage. You don't have to be a brain surgeon to be a brewer. But," he quickly adds, "it's hot, hard work." Nor is brewing a quick road to riches. "We're not making skads of money," Andy phrases it. Still Andy Hazen clearly enjoys making beer. Creating his own blends. And hearing people ask for an "Andy's."

ANDREW'S AT A GLANCE
Sold first beer = 1/93. 1995 production = 300 barrels (100% draught). Employees = 1. Major brands = Andrew's Brown Ale, Andrew's Old English Ale, Andrew's St. Nick Porter, Ruby's Golden Pale Ale. Available in select locations in central, southern, and mid-coast Maine. For directions and tour/tasting info call (207) 763-3305.

Andy Hazen, November 1995. When I asked Andy what has made him the happiest in his three-year career as a brewer, he replied "Just still being in business." It's not a bad answer.

Photo, August 1995, showing both the brewery, left, and the cafe, right. One of the things Doug especially likes about the micro-brewery business is its financial sense of scale. It's small. As he reflected: "If I wanted to get into steel I couldn't exactly open a micro-steel plant."

ATLANTIC BREWING COMPANY/LOMPOC CAFE & BREW PUB
30-36 RODRICK STREET, BAR HARBOR 04609

The first time Doug Maffucci heard the name "Acadia" he said "Where's that?" That was January 1975, while the Cross River, New York native was a student at Colby. A friend had suggested a camping trip and, even though he had no idea where he was going, Doug went... and loved it. In fact, he loved it so much he decided, then and there, that Mount Desert Island was going to be a part of his future. Little did he realize he would go on to become an MDI Beer Baron.

As with so many other Maine micro proprietors, however, Doug's route to brewing was a circuitous one. After graduating from Colby in 1978, Doug made his way to Portland to work as a carpenter and plasterer. One of his customers was the storied Alan Eames, founder of the equally storied Three Dollar Dewey's. Doug and the rest of the Dewey's construction crew would work from 3:00 pm to 11:00 pm... and then repair to Alan's for dinner and a round or two of the exotic brews for which Alan was - and is - famous. Says Doug without hesitation: "He was the one who showed me the great world of beers."

In 1980 it was bye bye, Portland / hello, Bar Harbor: Doug, with partner Jon Hubbard, opened a bicycle rental shop on Cottage Street. Three years later they added a hamburger joint, also on Cottage Street, to their "empire." Next, in 1987, came the purchase of a building complex on nearby Rodrick Street. "It was old and dilapidated," says Doug. But after two years of renovations - most of them done by Doug, Jon, and Doug's brother Chris - the complex was ready to rent. A small bistro opened. And failed. Doug and Jon and Chris decided to try their hand. They named their place the New Old Lompoc Cafe (after an eatery in a W.C. Fields' movie) and, harking back to Alan Eames, offered 25 bottled beer choices... none of them the usual run of national brands. It was pretty gutsy for its time - 1989 - but it succeeded. It wasn't enough for Doug, though: he'd visited his in-laws in Seattle that same year and had witnessed a world of micros galore. Doug resolved to bring a little of Seattle to Bar Harbor. He first hooked up with local home-brew maven Tod Foster (see Bar Harbor Brewing Company). The result was Tod's creation, Thunder Hole Ale, on tap at the New Old

Lompoc the summer of 1990. "It went over great," lauds Doug. But separate goals soon arose... and Doug and Tod went their separate ways. By 1991 Doug was doing his own brewing, initially within the Cafe and then, as the Acadia Brewing Company (changed to Atlantic Brewing Company as of January 1, 1994), in an adjoining part of the Rodrick Street complex.

Several expansions later, Doug is still going strong. And enjoying it. As he explained when I spoke with him in November 1995, "I like the idea of taking grain and making something out of it. And then coming into the pub and seeing someone enjoying a glass of your beer. It's," he concludes, "a very concrete, a very satisfying feeling."

ATLANTIC AT A GLANCE
Sold first beer = 5/91. 1995 production = 1,100 barrels (55% bottled / 45% draught). Employees = 23 (incl. restaurant). Major brands = Bar Harbor Real Ale, Bar Harbor Blueberry Ale, Lompoc's Ginger Wheat, Coal Porter. Available at select locations throughout Maine. For directions and tour/tasting info call (207) 288-9513.

Photo, November 1995. Doug in his Atlantic Brewing Company. It all began with a camping trip to Acadia National Park.

Photo, August 1995. If this looks like a house… that's because it is. Suzi and Tod and their daughter Meaghan live here. Upstairs. In the basement is a brewery. Plus there's a separate tasting and gift shop building out back.

BAR HARBOR BREWING COMPANY
ROUTE 3, OTTER CREEK ROAD, BAR HARBOR 04609

Mix one part Marin County, California and one part Bar Harbor, Maine and what do you get? The answer, for Tod and Suzi Foster at least, is a brewery.

Tod Foster was California all the way. He was born just north of San Francisco in 1953, graduated from the University of California at Santa Barbara in 1975, and was working for the National Marine Fisheries Service in San Diego. "I," he laughs, "was going to be Jacques Cousteau." Then he met Suzi Murphy in 1983. She was a born-(in 1954)-and-raised Bar Harborite who was studying at San Diego State.

"I had gone to San Diego," she, too, laughs, "to see what the real world was like." She wasn't impressed. By the time she and Tod met she was ready to go back to Bar Harbor. In September of 1983 she and Tod flew to Maine for a friend's wedding. The weather was great and Tod, suffering from slow career advancement and high-housing-cost blues, took especial note of Maine's real estate. "Hey," said he, "I could buy a whole island for what it would cost for a one-bedroom condo in a bad part of San Diego!" Suzi and Tod moved to Bar Harbor in May 1984.

Settled in Maine, Tod rekindled an old flame. He had homebrewed at the tender age of seven or eight - with his dad - and had homebrewed in college, too. In Maine he found he had the space to homebrew again. And by 1986 he was fashioning a dream: to own and operate a small brewery in Bar Harbor. It was a dream, however, that lay dormant until late 1989 when Tod ran across an ad for small-scale brewing equipment... and Suzi said "Are we going to do this or just talk about it forever?" They decided to do it.

Tod and Suzi first brewed for Doug Maffucci and his New Lompoc Cafe (see pages 118-119) in the summer of 1990. It went well but it was not what they wanted. What they wanted was a "farm brewery." And they took their first step toward it in 1991 when they ordered larger-scale equipment and moved operations to their home on Forest Avenue in downtown Bar Harbor.

From there - Forest Avenue is in a residential neighborhood and at tour time, recounts Tod, "There were cars all over and parked on peoples' lawns" - it was a logical move, in December 1992, to where Tod and Suzi are now, in a home on the outskirts of town. They raise some chickens and do some gardening and brew some beer. While they've grown, they're very proud of not allowing bigness to assume control. They're mindful of being successful... and yet small. "We were told we couldn't be successful on a small scale," states Tod, "but we are. We've carved out a certain lifestyle... and we love it."

BAR HARBOR AT A GLANCE
Sold first beer = 7/90. 1995 production = 250 barrels (100% bottled). Employees = 2½. Major brands = Thunder Hole Ale, Cadillac Mountain Stout, Harbor Lighthouse Ale, Bar Harbor Peach Ale. Available in select stores in central and southern Maine. For directions and tour/tasting info call (207) 288-4592.

Photo, November 1995. When I asked Tod and Suzi if they could conjure up a zany pose, Tod laughed and said he'd always wanted to pretend their brew kettle (sans the brew, of course) was a hot tub. And he climbed right on in. Suzi followed. Pretty zany.

Photo, November 1995. Milos picked the word "Bear" for the name of his brewpub because one evening he was playing Scrabble with his kids and that word was used and the kids liked it. "Basically, they picked it out," smiles Milos.

BEAR BREWPUB
35 MAIN STREET, ORONO 04473

There's Belgrade, Maine. And there's Belgrade, Yugoslavia. Milos Blagojevic comes from Belgrade, Yugoslavia. He is definitely "from away."

Born in 1953, Milos (pronounced "Meal-ous") grew up in an atmosphere of beer. His maternal grandmother was a brewer. "Our house was sort of the neighborhood brewery," laughs Milos. Nevertheless, Milos grew up with a desire to be in the forest service. He studied forestry at Belgrade University and then, after a stint in the army, went back to school for wildlife management and conservation. In 1978 he spent a year in the U.S.A, in Ithaca, New York, as an exchange student. While in

Ithaca he met a Cornell student, named Bonnie Haines, who would become his wife. The result was a teeter-totter existence for the next four years: time in Yugoslavia; time in the U.S.; etc. Finally, in June of 1982, Milos moved to America to stay. First stop was again Ithaca. In 1983, though, he landed a position as a forest engineer for the State of Maine and he and Bonnie settled in Orono.

Milos liked America. And Orono. After awhile, though, he tired of the life of a forest engineer. "Too much travel; too much time away from home," he explains. Milos became a real estate salesman, a job he held through 1994. It, too, did not totally fulfill him. "I was always looking to make some kind of product," he puts it. He found himself looking at commercial property with the thought in mind of starting some kind of business. What kind he didn't know. But some kind of business.

In 1992 Milos gambled and bought the building that now houses the Bear Brewpub. It had been home to, at one time or another, a hair salon, a flower shop, a bike repair shop, a storage facility. It was about 80 years old. And, relates Milos, it was "all dilapidated." Still, it was a start. And its size and location fit in well with an idea that had begun to come into focus the year before: the idea of, you guessed it, a brewpub. "I was always," notes Milos, "interested in beer and when we traveled I noticed these micros and how they were coming out with different types of beer." A talk with Alan Pugsley - dean of

Maine brewmasters - led to Milos taking a how-to-brew course at Alan's Kennebunkport Brewing Company in the fall of 1994. At the same time Milos was renovating his building and rounding up the necessary equipment.

The Bear Brewpub opened for business on September 1, 1995. "It was a dream come true," Milos beams. And, while business hasn't, Milos told me when we talked in November 1995, "been smashing," he's delighted at how much he and his staff have achieved in the two months since the opening. "And," he adds, "more people are coming in every day."

BEAR BREW AT A GLANCE
Sold first beer = 9/95. 1995 production = 84 barrels (100% draught). Employees = 11 (incl. restaurant). Major brands = Honey Bear Brown, I'll Be Darned Amber Ale, Midnight Stout, Great Works Blonde. Available only at Bear Brewpub. For directions and tour/tasting info call (207) 866-BREW.

Milos serving up a beer at the Maine Brewers' Festival, November 1995. He describes himself - with respect to his venture - as "owner/brewmaster/janitor." When I asked him if he missed Yugoslavia, he replied, "No. I found a home here."

Photo, May 1996. Formerly Patrick's Restaurant, the building that houses the Belfast Bay Brewing Company/Port Authority Brewpub – as well as the Ice Cream Barn & Family Restaurant – has been constructed over numerous stages and additions since 1971. Pat selected the name "Port Authority" because, as he explains, "Our theme inside our pub will be all the information about all the interesting things that have happened around the Belfast Bay area. So we're going to be, theoretically, the authority on the Port of Belfast." Pat's also going to be an authority on Maine beer: in addition to ten or so of his own brews, he intends to feature ten or so brews from other area micros. All on draught.

BELFAST BAY BREWING CO./THE PORT AUTHORITY BREWPUB
ROUTE 1 EAST, BELFAST 04915

Do ice cream and beer mix? The answer, for Pat Mullen at least, appears to be "Yes." Pat – real name = John Patrick Mullen – was born in Millinocket in 1941. His dad was a police officer, though, and Pat got to see a lot of Maine courtesy of his father's career moves. Patten, Island Falls, Houlton. Pat lived in them all before graduating from Enoch Crosby High in Belfast in 1960. He then attended Colby for two-plus years before open heart surgery cut short his stay on campus.

After recovering from his surgery, Pat was drawn to Massachusetts. "To earn my fame and fortune," he phrases it. His ticket was insurance: Pat and an associate opened a John Hancock agency in Brookline. But Pat and his wife Brenda – his sweetheart from high school

days in Belfast – ventured back to Maine every weekend. To a cottage on Swan Lake, just north of Belfast. Part of their weekend ritual was gassing up at Keswick's Store on Route 1 every Sunday before their return to the Bay State. Then one day it happened: there was a sign on the store that said "For Sale." Pat asked "How much?," thought about it for a day or so and decided to do it: vacate Massachusetts and his business and buy the store. That was 1970.

Within a year Pat and Brenda bought a parcel of land next to the store. It's the parcel that's now home to the Belfast Bay Brewing Company. Almost immediately the couple built a structure they called "The Barn" on their new property. It was a structure built to satisfy a desire... a desire for ice cream. "I was an ice cream freak,"

Pat explains, "and there was a little place in North Reading (Massachusetts) where I used to stop for ice cream all the time. One day the owner gave me his formulas because I was his best customer." Recalls Pat: "I said 'I'll never use these because it makes five gallons at a time and who's going to make five gallons of ice cream?'" With "The Barn" in place, however, Pat decided it was time to make use of those formulas. Mullen's Old Fashioned Ice Cream was born. At first the operation was take-out only, with hot dogs, hamburgers, and Mullen's Old Fashioned the banner sellers. But expansion beckoned. First indoor seating. Then waitresses. Then a lounge and alcoholic beverages.

Their success in Belfast led Pat and Brenda to open ice cream shops in Ellsworth and Bar Harbor, too. Via Bar Harbor Pat met Doug Maffucci. The two of them would sometimes daydream. One of the daydreams was about making beer. For Doug the dream came true in 1991 (please see pages 118-119). For Pat it's taken a little longer. After flirting with retirement for a time, Pat decided – in December of 1995 – to proceed with the business of beer. With Doug as consultant it's been "go" for Belfast Bay since. When I spoke with Pat in May he was shooting for a mid-June 1996 gala opening… with brand names the likes of Turtlehead Ale and Dark Harbor Porter. "And," I asked him, "will Mullen's Old Fashioned Ice Cream still be sold, too?" "You bet!," he answered unequivocally.

BELFAST BAY AT A GLANCE
As of press date, Belfast Bay's "glance" involves a look into the future. But by year's end Pat hopes to be brewing ten ales to be sold on premise and to be available at other bars and restaurants, too. Bottling is also envisioned in the relatively near future. For directions and updated info call (207) 338-4216.

Photo, May 1996. Having scored a success in ice cream, Pat hopes to do the same with beer. He sees similarities. Both can be handmade in small batches. Both have many admirers. Both offer an opportunity to be creative. Pat has 28 flavors of ice cream. His plans call for ten or so "flavors" of ale. And he's excited about developing – "inventing," if you will – those flavors. "My idea," he sums up, "is to make something special, and have people come to my place of business and say 'What you make is really good.'"

Photo, April 1996. It's a two-story, eight-room colonial where Neil and Lee and their children Emily and Adam and Andrew reside. But it's also the Berwick Brewing Company. For the time being, at least, Neil is still working full-time at the Portsmouth Navy Yard and doing his brewing on weekends. Who knows, though, what the future will bring?

BERWICK BREWING COMPANY
105 WILD ROSE LANE, SOUTH BERWICK 03908

For now, at least, it's Maine's most exclusive brew… like a private label that's very private. It's the brew created by the Berwick Brewing Company. As of this writing - May 1996 - it's available in only one place in the entire world, the Cape Neddick Inn (located on Route 1 in Cape Neddick). And that's just the way Neil and Lee Bryant, co-proprietors of Berwick Brewing, want it. "We don't want to worry about how much beer we put out," explains Neil. "We want to concentrate on quality and service and then worry about expanding."

A native of Lynn and Saugus, Massachusetts, Neil graduated from the University of Lowell with a degree in chemical engineering in 1985. He's been working as a nuclear engineer at the Portsmouth Navy Yard ever since. At age 27, in 1988, he began to dabble in home brew. Almost from his first batch he knew that someday he'd likely end up making beer *for sale,* too. That likelihood became stronger each time there were rumors of the Navy Yard closing. "Basically," recounts Neil, "I kept looking at what I wanted to do if the Yard closed." The only answer – repeatedly – was to brew beer.

The Yard hasn't closed. In fact it now appears to be on solid footing. Still Neil wanted to brew. In the fall of 1994 he and Lee decided to give it a shot part-time. They talked with other Maine brewers and began the road to licensing approval. By the fall of 1995 all signals were go… and the couple tackled the process of turning their home, built in 1989-1990, into a home *and* brewery. What used to be a garage is now a brewhouse. "We stole a portion of the basement, too," laughs Neil.

Neil has focused on perfecting a line-up of three brews: a brown ale (the couple's "flagship beer"), a stock ale, and a maple porter (porter with a small amount of maple syrup that leads, Neil assured me, to a taste that's both "very complex" and "interesting"). One other decision was to concentrate on a single account to start with. There was never any doubt which account Neil and Lee wanted that to be. The Cape Neddick. "We love their food," states Neil. "And," he adds, "we got married there… so it has a little history for us." After taste-testing a batch of Neil's beer, Cape Neddick management decided they liked the idea, too.

Result: Berwick's brews were the featured – and only! – brews on draught when the Inn opened for the season of 1996 in April. And, it's nice to be able to report, Cape Neddick's proprietor Glenn Gobeille plans on keeping the brewery's beers as his only on-tap choices for the foreseeable future. Both of the brewery's "parents" are, needless to say, delighted. Lee, perhaps, says it best: "It's kind of a neat business. People seem really interested in our beer. And receptive of it. And," she fairly glows, "I'm proud that we took it - brewing - from a hobby to a business."

BERWICK AT A GLANCE
Sold first beer = 4/96. 1995 production = 0 barrels. Employees = 2. Major brands = Berwick Brown Ale, Berwick Stock Ale. Available only at the Cape Neddick Inn in Cape Neddick. For directions and tour/tasting info call (207) 384-5847.

Photo, January 1996. A love of beer led Neil down the homebrewing path in 1988. He yet recalls those early days when he'd foist his test brews on friends and relatives and they'd try it and say "Hey, this really tastes like beer." Lee, a native of Chelsea and Medford, Massachusetts and a 1980 Salem State grad, is a corporate accountant by trade. She's the partnership's paperwork maven.

Photo, December 1995. Bray's is located in the circa 1880 former Epicurean Restaurant. "Charming" is the word Michele uses to describe it. Few would disagree.

BRAY'S BREWPUB & EATERY
ROUTES 302 AND 35, P.O. BOX 548, NAPLES 04055

"Naples Noses Out 99 Other Hoppy Hopefuls" could easily have been a headline in *The Bridgton News* in July 1995. It wasn't. But Mike Bray and Michele Windsor did check out a good 100 sites before they chose Naples as *the* site for themselves and their brewpub.

Were either Mike or Michele from Naples? Nope. Mike was born (in 1955) and raised in New Jersey. Michele was born (in 1959) in California and raised in Massachusetts. They met in Maine, while both were attending Nasson College in Springvale in the early 1980s. Their route to Naples was not to be a direct all-Maine route, though. Married in 1985, the couple spent the next nine years in Washington state, where Mike was an environmental chemist working with the federal government to mitigate hazardous waste sites. "I liked the job; I hated the politics," he says without hesitation. Bubbling in the back-

ground was brewing. Mike admits to having always had a fondness for beer. Good beer. In 1989 he began to translate this interest into homebrewing the best beer he could create. Friends gave him plenty of encouragement. "Everybody really liked my beers," he states unabashedly. "They couldn't wait for me to make more." Finally, after enough promises of "I'd buy this if it were for sale," Mike decided to get serious about trading environmental chemistry for brewing. First, however, he had to convince Michele. It wasn't easy. What did it was that she had a dream as well. That dream was to return to New England. "If you're going to quit your high-paying job," said she, "I want my wish, too."

With New England - and specifically Maine, where Michele had close friends from college - as their hoped-for Shangrila, the couple immersed themselves in location research, investigating sites in five states: Washington, Oregon, Idaho, New Hampshire and, of course, Maine. They came close with a former theatre in Kellogg, Idaho. But Maine kept calling. Finally, in May 1994, a Naples realtor sent a batch of Lake Region property-for-sale photos. Included was a circa 1880 Victorian home and barn turned gourmet restaurant. "Wow," said Michele, "This is beautiful." Four months later, in September, she and Mike came to Maine and she, at least, still said "Wow." Now it was Mike who had to be convinced. Demographics on Lake Region income and education helped. D.O.T. traffic counts (an average of 10,000 cars a day in 1994!) helped more. Of greater significance, though, was that Naples was, plain and simple, a place where Mike and Michele felt they'd like to live and raise a family. They liked the fact there was no other brewpub or micro nearby, either. "We wanted to be the only brewpub in the area," states Mike. Still, laughs

Michele, "Michael found it hard to believe that the best location was 3,000 miles away."

Mike and Michele entered into a lease/purchase agreement for their Naples "baby" on July 5, 1995. It was the day before their 10th wedding anniversary. Neither celebration - anniversary or agreement - lasted long: the couple, with immeasurable help from Mike's brother Rich, immediately began work turning dreams into realities. They took over operation of the restaurant on August 15th. Far more important, they poured their first for-sale-to-the-public beer on December 22nd. "Elated" is the word Mike uses to describe how he feels about seeing his dream come true. It's a good word.

BRAY'S AT A GLANCE
Sold first beer = 12/95. 1995 production = 4 barrels (100% draught). Employees = 5 full-time / 10 part-time (incl. restaurant). Major brands = Bray's Brandy Pond Blonde Wheat, Bray's Old Church Pale Ale, Bray's Pleasant Mountain Porter. Available only at Bray's. For directions and tour/tasting info call (207) 693-6806.

Mike and Michele, December 1995. Mike, as brewmaster, oversees the brewing side of Bray's. Michele doubles as restaurant manager and business manager. Aide-de-camp to both is their five-year old son, Mackenzie.

Photo, August 1995. While their brewery is named "Casco Bay," Mike and Bob's beer is named "Katahdin." "That name - Katahdin - represents to me the essence of Maine," states Mike. "It's a meaningful place... a place that represents northern Maine and wilderness."

CASCO BAY BREWING COMPANY
57 INDUSTRIAL WAY, PORTLAND 04103

It's only fitting and proper that Mike LaCharite is a brewer: after all, his father and grandfather and great-grandfather before him were all homebrewers. "It's in my blood," explains Mike.

Nevertheless, owning and operating a brewery in the State of Maine was not exactly what Mike had in mind when he graduated from Brunswick (Maine) High School in 1978. "I wanted to get out of Maine and see the world," he laughs. So Mike, born and raised in Brunswick, joined the Navy and spent four years "seeing the world" working with radar and electronics in California. He then joined a Los Angeles-area computer firm named

Datagraphix, working for them for an even dozen years, from 1982 to 1994. Early on, though, Mike moved his base of operations back to Maine, setting up a Datagraphix branch office in Bangor (later Topsham) in 1985. Nineteen eighty-five was a watershed year for Mike in another way as well: an old Brunswick High buddy gave him a few bottles of his homebrew. Mike liked what he tasted, felt the stirrings of his forefathers... and decided to try his hand at homebrew, too.

From ground zero Mike progressed rapidly. He liked his first batch and just kept on brewing. And reading about brewing. Almost before he knew it, in 1986, he entered the Common Ground Fair's homebrew competition where he won a blue ribbon for both of the beers he submitted. More ribbons and the founding of M.A.L.T. (Maine Ale & Lager Tasters), a statewide homebrewers' club, followed. So did the realization, circa 1991, that he could and should turn his penchant for brewing into a business. Mike's Plan A was to open a brewpub in his hometown of Brunswick but, before he'd gone very far down that road he realized a brewpub would involve him in the restaurant business… and that was a business in which he didn't want to be involved. "I didn't want to worry whether a waitress was cute enough or a hamburger was cooked right," he laughs again. "I just wanted to be a brewer."

Four years later that's just what Mike is: a brewer. It took three rather ardous years to get everything in order, but it was all worthwhile when, in June of 1994, Mike brewed his first batch of commercial beer. Not in Brunswick, either, but in a 5,000 square-foot facility in Portland's Turnpike Industrial Park. It's a building that "fit our needs" Mike states as he tells why he abandoned his Brunswick aspirations. With him in the venture is partner Bob Wade, a 48-year old Portland/South Portland/Saco native and Dartmouth grad who left a successful career with Hannaford Bros. to join Mike in 1993. Mike handles the brewing end; Bob the business end. It's a good fit. Sums up Mike: "Brewing is a great, industry. I can't think of anything I'd rather do."

CASCO BAY AT A GLANCE

Sold first beer = 8/94. 1995 production = 4,000 barrels (80% bottled / 20% draught). Employees = 4 full-time/ 3 part-time. Major brands = Katahdin Red Ale, Katahdin Golden Beer, Katahdin Stout. Available in 10 states in New England, New Jersey, and the Midwest. For directions and tour/tasting info call (207) 797-2020.

Mike, left, and Bob having a good time at the Maine Brewers' Festival, November 1994. The partners met in 1993 while Mike was teaching a homebrew course at the Whip & Spoon in Portland. Bob was a student. "We," says Mike, "hit it off right away."

Photo, August 1995. Located in Portland's Evergreen Industrial Park, Maine's pioneer micro brewery was built to be functional, not beautiful. "We looked around before we constructed it," says David, "and we looked at some older buildings… but the problem with old buildings is that they're old buildings." David sums up his facility by calling it "perfect for us."

D.L. GEARY BREWING COMPANY
38 EVERGREEN DRIVE, PORTLAND 04103

When I introduced David Geary to my son Curt at the 1995 Maine Brewers' Festival I introduced him as "The Grandfather of Maine Brewers." David smiled and simply said, "I prefer 'Dean." "Dean" or "Grandfather" or "Old Brew Eyes" (another sobriquet sometimes used), David Geary has - by Maine brewing standards - been brewing beer in Maine a long, long time.

Born in Portland in 1945, David graduated from Deering High and then shuffled off to Indiana where he attended Purdue on what he jokingly terms "the nine year plan." By that he means he met and married the former Karen Kramer (also a Purdue student) and they had a baby. Result: he attended school when he could afford it and worked when he couldn't. After finally garner-

ing a B.A. in 1972, David (and Karen and daughter Kelly) settled in Portland. David found employ as a pharmaceutical salesman, covering Maine and New Hampshire for Abbott Labs. After seven years he switched firms, joining the George C. Frye Company as a medical equipment salesman. "I did well at it," recounts David, "but I couldn't see myself going into the sunset doing the same thing forever."

By 1983 - when Frye went bankrupt - David knew he was ready for a change. And he knew it was to brewing… an idea that had been hatching since David and Karen had met Alan Eames, founder of Three Dollar Dewey's, in 1981-1982. "It was Alan who started the idea of a micro brewery in my head," David is quick to admit. His future was sealed when he also met Peter Maxwell Stuart, owner of a brewery in Scotland. Peter offered David an apprenticeship at his brewery. David gladly accepted, spending six months learning the ways of traditional British ales in the winter/spring of 1984. He came back to the States ready and raring to go.

It would be marvelous to say that the D.L. Geary Brewing Company was a smash success right from its start. But it wouldn't be true. When you're first in line it's easy to make mistakes. "We operated in a vacuum," David phrases it. "There was no one else to turn to for help or information." If he and Karen ran out of hops they couldn't run to the brewery next door and borrow a cup. And when David called on a potential account he'd have to explain what he was doing… what a micro brewery is all about. He was once even asked: "Is your beer like Bud?" (David's answer: "Well, no. Absolutely not.").

It's been almost ten years since David and Karen sold their first beer (in December 1986, with Alan Pugsley as their brewmaster). No one asks David if his Geary's Pale Ale tastes like Bud anymore. He and Karen have divorced (and David's remarried), but they're still partners at the brewery even if they aren't "in real life." In fact, it's a family affair: daughter Kelly, 28, and son Matthew (when he's not in college), 21, both work at the brewery, too. As to "the sunset"… well, David's still in love with making beer. "There used to be a belief that beer," he tells me, "was God's gift to humanity." It's a belief David firmly adhers to. "Just bury me in a beer vat," he laughs, "with a sprig of hops clutched in my hand."

GEARY'S AT A GLANCE
Sold first beer = 12/86. 1995 production = 13,300 barrels (78% bottled / 22% draught). Employees = 12 full-time / 5 part-time. Major brands = Geary's Pale Ale, Geary's Hampshire Special Ale, Geary's London Porter, Geary's American Ale. Available from Maine south to South Carolina and west to Ohio. For directions and tour/tasting info call (207) 878-2337.

Photo, Kelly and David, February 1996. When the D.L. Geary Brewing Company opened in late 1986 it was the first micro in New England and one of less than 20 in the entire country. I commented to David that his opening was, therefore, pretty darned courageous. His reply: "It would have taken far more courage to have résumés printed and to have gone to work for someone else."
Kelly has worked at the brewery the last two years. "I love it," she told me. "I worked for law firms for nine years. This is a much more rewarding career."

Photo, August 1995. The Great Falls Brewing Company and its companion, No Tomatoes* Restaurant, occupy part of the ground floor of the majestic circa 1880 Goff Block in downtown Auburn.

GREET FALLS BREWING COMPANY
36 COURT STREET, AUBURN 04210

Cass Bartlett well recalls Great Falls' first brew. First brew sold, that is. It was just six minutes after midnight on February 11, 1994. "We had just become legal," Cass recounts, "and there was this older guy with a long white beard sitting at the bar. I asked him if he'd like to be customer number one and he said he would." Cass smiles as he tells how the old gentleman enjoyed an amber. And then enjoyed a second amber. And then disappeared. "I haven't seen him before or since," continues Cass as he smiles even more. "I figure maybe he was a 'brewer's god' who came down to oversee the opening of the brewpub… and then went merrily on his way."

Brewer's god or not, Cass has traveled a zig zag line to Auburn and brewing. Born and raised in Chelmsford, Massachusetts, the now 46-year old brewer fell in love with Maine as a 14-year old when he spent a summer helping to restore a house in Kingfield. The result was that he talked his parents into sending him to Kents Hill School, from which he graduated in 1968. From there it was on to Monmouth College in Monmouth, Illinois and then the University of Maine at Orono. While in college Cass became enamored of theatre, and before his final curtain call he performed in Boston, Portland, and throughout New England. From the stage he moved on to Bar Harbor, where he served as Activity Director at Summit House Center from

1980 to 1985, and to varied sales jobs into the 1990s.

Ever-present in the background, though, was a love of beer and the realization that there was beer... and there was good beer. "I remember I had a Wurzburger Dark sometime around 1972 or so," recalls Cass, "and I said to myself 'Why doesn't America brew beer like this?" It was a question that caused Cass to begin experimenting with his own homebrew and to follow the micro awakening with more than just a casual interest. "That this - the brewing of beers of merit - was beginning to happen in the U.S. was like a fantasy coming true," is how Cass puts it. His own contribution to the fantasy began in late 1992. Cass had gone to UMO with Charlie

Herrick, co-proprietor (with Mike Colerick) of No Tomatoes Restaurant in Auburn. At a 40th birthday bash for Charlie the conversation turned to beer. Charlie said he was giving some thought to building a micro into No Tomatoes... but really didn't know much about it. Cass said that he did and that he had some capital and that he'd be interested in doing the brewing. The rest, as they say, is history.

When I interviewed Cass in October 1995 - twenty months after the "brewer's god" had partaken of that initial Great Falls Amber - he was most definitely upbeat. "I work 60-65 hours a week and my social life is hell," he relays, "but the payoff is when I come out into the restaurant area and I see people are relaxing and having a good time drinking the beer I made. That's the payoff. It makes it all worthwhile." Then he added a few words that you can't help but love: "Instead of labor it's excitement."

GREAT FALLS AT A GLANCE
Sold first beer = 2/94. 1995 production = 310 barrels (100% draught). Employees = 4. Major brands = Bobcat Brown Ale, Mad Dog Porter, Great Falls Amber Ale, Court Street Raspberry Wheat. Available at Great Falls/No Tomatoes* and select locations in southern Maine. For directions and tour/tasting info call (207) 795-0277.

*PLEASE NOTE: AS OF MID-MAY 1996 WHAT WAS NO TOMATOES RESTAURANT BECAME THE COURT HOUSE TAVERN, UNDER NEW PROPRIETORS PAUL AND KATE LANDRY, AND SCOTT AND ROBIN McFARREN. GREAT FALLS, THOUGH, LIVES ON (WITH CASS STILL DOING THE BREWING) AND WILL PROVIDE BEER TO BOTH COURT HOUSE AND TO AN INCREASED LINE-UP OF OTHER LOCATIONS IN CENTRAL AND SOUTHERN MAINE.

Photo, October 1995. A love of relative lack of population brought Cass Bartlett to Maine. A love of good beer led him to brewing.

Photo, October 1995. For the story of how the name "Gritty McDuff" came to be, please see page 138.

GRITTY McDUFF'S BREWPUB
LOWER MAIN STREET, FREEPORT 04032

It took an Aussie, a Yankee, and a tropical paradise to hatch the idea that became Gritty's. But hatch it did. The Aussie was an unknown shipyard worker; the tropical paradise was Waikiki; the Yankee was - and is - Richard Pfeffer.

Actually, Richard isn't a true Yankee. He was born in Rochester, New York. In 1964. But his family moved to Litchfield, Connecticut in 1967. And Richard moved with them. Ten years later the family and Richard moved to Freeport. After graduation from the Brooks School in North Andover, Massachusetts, Richard went back to upstate New York, to the University of Rochester, graduating with a B.A. in 1985. His goal at the time was Wall Street. The world of high finance. But after a few interviews he asked himself if finance was really what he wanted. The answer came back "No."

Richard, instead, took a year to travel. To "see the world." It was fortuitous. A motorcycle ride across Canada and down the U.S. west coast led to work aboard a boat out of San Diego and from there to a job repairing a ship in Waikiki. It was there, while sharing the secrets of life with a fellow ship repairman, that Richard mentioned he was thinking of going back to Maine and opening a bar. The fellow ship repairman - who Richard recalls as "a young and sort of restless kind of guy" hailing from Brisbane - said "Why don't you make it a brewpub?"

That was early in 1986. Richard thought a brewpub was a great idea. But it was an idea he wasn't ready to put in motion. He did, though, return to Maine in June 1986 and signed on as a stockbroker for Winslow Investment. But the idea of a brewpub wouldn't go away. From late 1987-on Richard found himself spending more thought on a brewpub business plan than on stocks and bonds. "I felt guilty," he admits. In April of 1988 Richard parted company with Winslow and went brewpub full time. The result was the opening of Gritty's/Portland on July 27, 1988 and the pouring of Gritty's own first brew on December 21st. (For more on Gritty's/Portland see the next two pages.).

Not a man to rest on his laurels, Richard began to think of Gritty's II even before the beer mats were worn at Gritty's I. He and his associates looked into Portsmouth and Manchester, New Hampshire, Newport, Rhode Island, Boston, and Bangor and Bar Harbor. "In the back of my head, though, I always thought that Freeport would be a good location," says Richard. He liked its proximity to the mother Gritty's (feel-

ing it would be easier to manage two locations if they weren't too far apart) and the fact that "4,000,000 people come to Freeport each year and they have to eat and drink somewhere."

Freeport moved into the realm of possibility in early 1994 and became a certainty with the leasing of the brewpub's location in April. Opening Day was July 21st. Asked how he felt that grand day, Richard replied "Relieved." The whole process, replete with financing, licensing, leasing, and partnership problems, had been much more difficult than ever envisioned. Since then, though, things have sailed along at a smoother pace. When I spoke with Richard in November 1995 he used the word "excellent" to describe the happenings since the opening. "The opportunities, " he added, "are increasing exponentially."

GRITTY'S / FREEPORT AT A GLANCE
Sold first beer = 6/95. 1995 production = 644 barrels (100% draught). Employees = 68 (incl. restaurant). Major brands = Gritty McDuff's Best Bitter, Gritty McDuff's Best Brown Ale, Gritty McDuff's Black Fly Stout. Available at select locations throughout New England and in upstate New York. For directions and tour/tasting info call (207) 865-4321.

Richard, right and the Stebbins' cousins, Bill, left, and Ed, center, looking good at the Maine Brewers' Festival, November 1995. Ed is brewmaster at Gritty's/Portland while Bill does the honors at Freeport.

Photo, October 1995. There is or was no "Gritty McDuff." It's a made-up name, the output of founder Richard Pfeffer's fertile imagination. "I wanted a name with a British identity," he explains. The "Gritty" part came from an old high school buddy named Sandy MacLeod. "Somehow, 'Sandy' got converted to 'Gritty,'" Richard laughs. "McDuff" just arrived out of the blue one day. Everybody liked it, so Richard went with it even though he, himself, was not particularly fond of it. "It's a little too silly, too fabricated," he feels. But it's a name that's here to stay. As Richard says: "It's catchy. And it works."

GRITTY McDUFF'S
396 FORE STREET, PORTLAND 04101

I had awarded the "from away" award to Milos Blagojevic of the Bear Brewpub in Orono. Milos is, after all, from Belgrade, Yugoslavia, 4244 air miles away. Then I ran into Ed Stebbins, brewmaster and co-proprietor of Gritty's. Ed was born in 1962 in Buenos Aires, Argentina. It is 5441 air miles away. Ed wins the award.

What was Ed doing in Buenos Aires? Well, his father was stationed there at a branch of the Bank of Boston. Ed and family bounced around South America until 1975 , when his dad was transferred to London. "I tagged along," laughs

Ed. In 1980 he finally came to North America. To Maine, where he attended Hebron Academy for a year. Then it was off to Oneonta, in upstate New York, where Ed went to Hartwick College, graduating with a B.A. in 1985. While at Hartwick, Ed involved himself in the restaurant business: he toiled as a waiter and bartended and worked his way up to manager of the college's coffee house. He's proud that he introduced pioneer microbrewer Bill Newman's Albany Amber Ale to the coffee house. "It tasted like a true English ale," reflects Ed. And Ed knew his English ale: in London he and his family lived next door to a brewery.

An even more lasting legacy from Oneonta days is Ed's wife, Audrey. They met at Hartwick and after graduation spent several years "just bumming around," as Ed describes it. The couple then decided to "get serious," settling in Boston where Ed worked at the Museum of Fine Arts. Audrey, however, much preferred Maine to Boston. "She was drawn to it," laughs Ed. Eventually, she drew Ed to it, too. They moved to Vacationland in January 1987.

In Portland, Ed found himself part of an exciting birthing process. He and Richard Pfeffer had been friends since college days. Richard and two associates wanted to open a brewpub but, as Ed phrases it rather undelicately, "They didn't know what a brewpub was." Nor did they have the necessary capital. Ed solved the latter by talking his grandmother into lending him a fair chunk of money. With money in hand Ed joined the venture as a full-fledged partner. Ed also solved the-lack-of-experience problem by apprenticing under Alan Pugsley and David Geary at Geary's. Ed is especially appreciative of the support offered by David: "He went out of his way to help us, both as a fellow brewer and as a businessman."

With Ed at the helm as brewmaster, Gritty's offered up its first "official" brew on December 21, 1988. "It wasn't really that good," admits Ed. "Our heart was in it, though, and Portland responded in kind… they took us into their heart."

In closing out our November 1995 interview, Ed stated he feels Gritty's beer is now "world class." And he told a story to illustrate how far he and his colleagues have come. In the very early days of the brewpub, a customer walked in and asked for a Budweiser. "I'm sorry, sir, but we only pour what we brew here," politely replied the bartender on duty. "Well, then," responded the customer, "brew me a Bud." Now customers, Ed proudly points out, "want the most exotic and esoteric beer styles we can brew."

GRITTY'S / PORTLAND AT A GLANCE
Sold first beer = 12/88. 1995 production = 4,336 barrels (64% bottled / 36% draught). Employees = 64 (incl. restaurant). Major brands = Gritty McDuff's Best Bitter, Gritty McDuff's Best Brown Ale, Gritty McDuff's Black Fly Stout. Available at select locations throughout New England and in upstate New York. For directions and tour/tasting info call (207) 772-2739.

Photo, November 1995. Ed and Audrey and their then-3½ month old son, James, at the Maine Brewers' Festival in Portland. When I asked Ed if he thought his son might someday become a brewmaster, he responded with an old Czech proverb: "Blessed be the mother who gives birth to a brewer."

Photo, August 1995. The Kennebunkport Brewing Company was opened in June of 1992. Alan's proud that the first three brews he developed for the brewery - Shipyard Export Ale, Goat Island Light, and Taint Town Pale Ale (the latter available at Federal Jack's only) - are still going strong. On a much grander scale, Alan's proud of his contributions to America's micro-brewing industry and, in turn, of all the jobs that industry has helped create.

KENNEBUNKPORT BREWING COMPANY / FEDERAL JACK'S BREW PUB
8 WESTERN AVENUE, KENNEBUNK 04043

Alan Pugsley smiles as he recalls June 16, 1986. It's the day he flew out of London's Gatwick Airport. Destination = Portland, Maine. "It was a pretty big move," he admits, "leaving England and family and friends behind to seek the excitement of America." Adds Alan: "With two suitcases in hand."

Born in Leamington Spa (near Stratford-on-Avon), England in 1959, Alan has been involved with brewing almost since his graduation from Manchester University with a degree in biochemistry in 1981. First stop was the Ringwood Brewery in Hampshire. There Alan learned the art and science of brewing under the watchful eye of noted brewer Peter Austin. To this day it's the training he received under Peter that Alan credits for his success. During his stay at Ringwood (1982-1985) Alan met a young David Geary. That was 1984 when

David was in Great Britain earning his stripes as a budding brewer. David mentioned his desire to open a brewery in Portland. Alan listened and said he might just be the man to help out. After David returned to the States the two kept in touch via letters. Eventually David offered Alan a job. Alan accepted.

Alan and David remained a team - at D.L. Geary - until November of 1988, when Alan went out on his own as a rep for Peter Austin's micro-brewing system. In the years since he's gone on to become, as one writer dubbed him, "The Johnny Appleseed of Brewing," with over 50 micro and brew pub start-ups in the U.S. and Canada to his credit.

In December 1991 Alan met Fred Forsley (please see pages 156-157). Within a month the two had struck a deal: Alan would oversee brewing activities at Fred's fledgling Kennebunkport Brewing Company and, in exchange, be able to make use of the brewery to demonstrate Peter Austin's equipment and to train people in the

use of it. Alan laughs as he remembers, fondly, the development of Kennebunkport's first brews...especially the development of Shipyard Export Ale. "Basically," he says, "I tried to brew a beer that tasted like what Molson's Ale would've tasted like 30 years ago."

Since January of 1994 Alan has been a partner in Shipyard and is heavily involved in Shipyard's brews both in Kennebunk and Portland. But he still - under the appellation Pugsley's Brewing Projects International - consults, too. He's justifiably quite happy. "I've found a great career and a great place - Maine and New England - to do it in," he says with vigor. "You'll find your pot of gold in America," David Geary had promised all those years ago. And, indeed, Alan Pugsley has.

KENNEBUNKPORT AT A GLANCE
Sold first beer = 6/92. 1995 production = 1430 barrels (98% draught / 2% bottled). Employees = 27 (incl. restaurant). Major brands = Shipyard Export Ale, Goat Island Light, Blue Fin Stout, Taint Town Ale. Available at Federal Jack's in Kennebunk. For directions and tour/tasting info call (207) 967-4311.

Photo, February 1996. With over 50 micro and brew pub start-ups to his credit (including Geary's, Gritty's, Sea Dog, and Sugarloaf) in North America, Alan has been called "the Johnny Appleseed of Brewing." "Of course, laughs the English native, "I had to ask who Johnny Appleseed was."

Carol and Dan McGovern's house and brewery, November 1995. The brewhouse sits in a sunroom in the rear of the house; conditioning and storage takes place in the basement.

LAKE ST. GEORGE BREWING COMPANY
FR 6, ROUTE 220/RR 1, BOX 2505, LIBERTY 04949

A game of volleyball forever changed the lives of Dan McGovern and Kellon Thames. "It was just a YMCA league in Belfast," laughs Kellon, but after the game one of the other players, who happened to be Dan, mentioned that he was a homebrewer. So was Kellon. "We became friends… and it (the Lake St. George Brewing Company) started from there."

Maine's brewers have come from all over. Even Maine. Kellon was born in Belfast in 1956, grew up in Liberty, and has two degrees - a B.S. and an M.B.A. - from the University of Maine, Orono. His original plan was to become a banker, a trade he practiced from 1984 to 1989. Then he burned out. Lurking in the background was beer. Kellon had taken a trip to England in 1983 and hung around with friends who were into making their own beer. "I ended up drinking a lot of bitter," he reminisces. He also bought his first homebrewing kit and brought it back on the plane with him. He's been brewing ever since.

Dan is not from Maine. He's from the heartland. He was born in Terre Haute in 1953 and raised in Indianapolis. His homebrewing roots stretch back to 1972 when he began to brew his own brew while a student in college. His introduction to Maine came four years later when he and his wife Carol came here for their honeymoon. Love, sweet love. Dan really liked Maine. And he and Carol came back several times on vacation trips before deciding, in 1982, to make Maine their home. The fact that Carol's grandfather lived in Liberty was a part of the decision. That Dan had a very transportable skill - he's a meatcutter - was another. In Indiana, Dan had worked for Kroger's Supermarkets. In Maine he joined the gang at Shop & Save, first in Belfast, and now in Rockland.

From volleyball to commercial brewing is not as easy as 1-2-3. After becoming friends, Dan and Kellon began to talk about the possibility of making beer for money. Their catalyst came in the form of Suzi and Tod Foster, Bar Harbor's brewing couple. Dan and Kellon visited Suzi and Tod in mid-1991, and came away encouraged, believing their own brewery, in Kellon's words, "was do-able." Suzi and Tod gave them nothing but support. "We're proof," said they, "that it doesn't have to cost $1,000,000."

For most of 1991 and 1992 Dan and Kellon talked and listened and researched. They were cautious because, as Kellon again puts it, "We thought we were getting into the tail end of what the state could support (in the way of

micros)." Kellon and Dan both get a hearty laugh out of that now.

By 1993 the duo was ready to roll. Dan and Carol added a 10' x 20' sunroom onto the rear of their home and Dan and Kellon transformed it into a brewery. Their first "public" brew went on the market on June 29th. At the Great Lost Bear in Portland. "It - the brew - was still a little rough at that point," admits Kellon. But he and Dan were delighted at the response… and have been delighted with the response ever since. They're also delighted with their own growth as brewers. "We learn from every new style," states Dan. "But is it fun?," I asked. "It's a mixture," he responded honestly. "It's kinda neat… but it takes plenty of hard work and dedication."

LAKE ST. GEORGE AT A GLANCE
Sold first beer = 6/93. 1995 production = 150 barrels (100% draught). Employees = 2. Major brands = Dirigo Brown Ale, Lake St. George Oatmeal Stout, Lake St. George Pale Ale. Available at select locations in southern, central, and mid-coast Maine. For directions and tour/tasting info call (207) 589-4180.

Kellon, left, and Dan at the Maine Brewers' Festival, November 1995. Both still hold down fulltime jobs: Dan as a meatcutter for Hannaford Bros. and Kellon as sales manager for Liberty Graphics. They get together to brew from one to three times a week, depending on the season and the demand.

Tom, right, who's 30, and brewmeister Nate Hills, left, who's 26, pose in front of their "baby," November 1995. Brother Dan is 26. Quipped Tom: "I'm the oldtimer in the bunch."

MAINE COAST BREWING COMPANY
21 COTTAGE STREET, BAR HARBOR 04609

You might say that Tom St. Germain and Bar Harbor ran - literally - into each other. "I was on the cross country team at college (William and Mary) and wanted a place that was cool during the summer so I could run and stay in shape," he told me during a November 1995 interview. The fact that Bar Harbor has no shortage of bars was a plus, too. Tom wanted to work in a bar. And, beginning in 1987 at the Parkside Restaurant on Main Street, that's just what he did.

From the beginning Tom was taken with the bar business and, after graduation from school

in 1989, the Chelmsford, Massachusetts native moved to Bar Harbor to live year around. He especially like Mount Desert Island's seasonality...that he could work half the year and be free to do whatever he wanted the other half. He could be "semi-retired," as he phrases it.

Tom used his "retirement" time, in the years 1989 through 1992, to write and self-publish three books on hiking and biking in Acadia. But he was restless. Working at the Parkside and being an MDI publishing mogul was fine... but what Tom really wanted was a pub of his own. And the idea of that pub being a brewpub

- a thought initially put forth by Tom's younger brother, Dan - grew ever stronger in intensity. By 1992 it was almost an obsession. "I looked at every conceivable commercial structure in Bar Harbor," he says, "including basements and second stories." Nothing felt right. That was the winter of 1992-1993. Ditto for the winter of 1993-1994. In the spring of 1994, somewhat in dispair, Tom signed on as a rep for Gritty McDuff's launch of its Best Bitter in bottles. His sales territory extended from Bar Harbor to Bangor to Rockland. One of the people he called on was Freddie Pooler, proprietor of Freddie's Route 66 Restaurant, located on Cottage Street in downtown Bar Harbor. When Tom mentioned that what he really wanted was his own brewpub, Freddie stepped up and said "Why don't you open it in my building?" It took Tom about six seconds to say "Okay." All was easier said than done, however: there followed a solid eight months of negotiation before all the details were worked out and Tom and Dan and brewmaster Nate Hills could roll. And roll they did, transforming the building Freddie had in mind - a smallish built-in-1987 former book store/former tee-shirt store/former jewelry store/former hamburger haven - into a real live brewpub. All the headaches, though,

became worthwhile on May 19th ... the day Tom and Dan and Nate flung open their doors to the thirsty throngs. Actually, it didn't really work that way. "The first six weeks were slow," recounts Tom. "It was scary." Then, seemingly overnight, things changed. "Business went from being terrible to being great." Tom credits the change to "good fortune," but admits the arrival of tourist season may have had something to do with it as well. He summed up our November interview by terming his first year's experience "great;" quickly adding "It made me really look forward to the future."

MAINE COAST AT A GLANCE
Sold first beer = 5/95. 1995 production = 233 barrels (95% draught / 5% bottled). Employees = 5 (incl. restaurant). Major brands = Bar Harbor Gold, Sweet Waters Stout, Eden Porter, Great Head Ale. Available at select locations in central, southern, and mid-coast Maine. For directions and tour/tasting info call (207) 288-4114.

In its inaugural year, 1995, Maine Coast Brewing sold its brews on draught and, uniquely, by the jug. Here's a shot of the jug.

Photo, May 1996. The Narrow Gauge Brewing company is nestled inside the Granary Brew Pub and Coffee House. The structure that houses both dates back to circa 1870. Home to Fiddleheads Restaurant from 1977 until 1995, it had previously long been occupied by a hardware store and was originally a granary. In fact the granary chutes are still in place, brewpub and coffee house proprietor Gary Guyette told me with obvious pride.

NARROW GAUGE BREWING CO./GRANARY BREW PUB
23 PLEASANT STREET, FARMINGTON 04938

Different people move to Maine for different reasons. For Carl Wegner it was snow. Born in New Jersey in 1950, Carl grew up in Windsor in upstate New York and then went to Lafayette College in Easton, Pennsylvania. There he garnered a degree in mechanical engineering in 1972. Carl then "dabbled," as he puts it, in engineering back in New York in 1973-74. But he didn't really take to it. "I wasn't suited for inside desk work, I found out," he says.

After studying geology for several years, Carl got into cross country skiing, as a participant and then as an occupation. From 1978 to 1982 he worked at The Inn at Starlight Lake in Starlight, Pennsylvania. While there he met – and married – the former Marilyn Lempke. By 1982 the couple realized there were better places to be in the "snow business" than Pennsylvania. Maine

seemed a logical location, and when they heard of an opening at Saddleback in Rangeley they decided to accept it. "We loaded all our worldly possessions in a U-Haul," says Carl, "and moved to the mountains of Maine."

For the next four years Carl cut and groomed trails, gave lessons, etc. That was during the winter. The rest of the year he and Marilyn held down a variety of other jobs. Quite a number of Carl's jobs involved carpentry, and by 1986 he felt proficient enough to trade skis et al. for hammer et al., forming his own construction company. Marilyn, meanwhile, was commuting to Farmington for coursework at UMF. It was a tough commute and, in the fall of 1987, the couple opted to move "down into civilization." They chose Wilton, where Carl continued with carpentry and construction.

In 1993 there occurred the event – events, actually – that started Carl on his road to beer "fame and fortune." For Christmas Marilyn bought him a homebrewing kit, while his mother Anna contributed a four-gallon stainless steel stock pot. The pot was meant for soupmaking but Carl put the two together and said "I think we have something here." As he laughs, "The brewing kit's instructions said 'Put a big pot on the stove' and here was the pot."

Brewing commenced almost immediately. "It – homebrewing – felt very natural and good," smiles Carl. "And the beer was good." Soon Carl and Marilyn were visiting commercial brewers around the state. "I could do this," Carl found himself saying. Marilyn wasn't so sure: she feared the Farmington/Wilton area wasn't populous enough and didn't have enough of a tourist base. Push almost came to shove in the spring of 1995 when the area's best-known eatery, Fiddleheads, was put up for sale. Carl, though, did nothing about it... except to dream

and tell his work buddies that "We ought to buy it and renovate it." Instead, local businessfolk Gary and Dale Guyette bought it... and promptly announced a brewpub was part of their renovation plans. In December the man who was going to be doing the brewing at the brewpub, however, backed out. Carl felt it was now or never. "If I don't do it I'm going to be miserable," he told Marilyn. She acquiesced. Carl talked with Gary and Dale. "I hear you need a brewer," he said "Ok," they said.

When I visited with Carl six months later, in May 1996, he had just shared his first commercial brews with the Farmington community. Three of his beers were on tap at Gary and Dale's Granery Brew Pub & Coffee House with plans for more on the way. I kidded him about whether people were coming up to him and asking for his autograph. He smiled and said, "No, not yet." But, he smiled again, "People do come up to me and ask 'How's the beer coming?' And what does Carl reply? Carl replies "Just great!"

NARROW GAUGE AT A GLANCE
Sold first beer = 5/96. 1995 production = 0. (Est. future production = 200 barrels a year). Employees = 1. Major brands = Iron Rail Ale, Clearwater Cream Ale, Sidetrack Ale. Available only at the Granery Brew Pub in Farmington. For directions and tour/tasting call (207) 778-5363 or 779-0710.

Photo, May 1996. Accustomed to being a master of many trades, Carl is presently juggling his beer life with his carpentry/construction life. For now, at least, he's brewing two days a week. The name "Narrow Gauge" honors the former Sandy River & Rangeley Lakes Railroad, a narrow gauge line that ran from Farmington to Strong, Bigelow, Rangeley and other far-flung Franklin County points. Reflects Carl: "I like railroads."

Photo, May 1996. Can a present-day brewery find happiness in a latter-day chicken barn? Sure. As Pat laughs: "It's a great big barn just dying to be a micro brewery." And with the unlikely team of a photographer (Pat), two research scientists (Trebor and Mike), and a Mary Kay representative (K.T.) – along with the very necessary ingredient of a brewer (Chris) – it should all happen in June and July 1996. The entire first floor of the barn – which weighs in at 2,600 square feet – is earmarked for Oak Pond, with two/thirds of it set aside for brewing and conditioning/kegging, and the other one/third set aside for the bottling operation that Pat, Chris et al. hope to have up and functioning before too many more suns have set over Skowhegan.

OAK POND BREWING COMPANY
OAK POND ROAD (OFF ROUTE 2, EAST), BOX 1208, SKOWHEGAN

"I liked the flavor. It was very different." So says Pat (Richardson) Lawton about the bottle of Geary's she drank in the spring of 1994. "I hadn't had a beer in years," she continues, "and suddenly I was awakened as to what was happening in the micro world." It was an awakening that was to change her life. Almost before Pat knew it she and her husband Trebor were deep into "all these statistics on the micro and brewpub industry" that Trebor kept bringing home. And then, again almost before she knew it, she and Trebor had decided they wanted to join in... to be a part of the industry.

Brewing beer was a long way from Pat's career path plans growing up in Skowhegan, where she was born in 1956. Her plan was art. She graduated from Purdue University – the alma mater, ironically, of both David and Karen Geary, too – with a degree in fine arts. Then, influenced by fellow-Purdue student and husband-to-be Trebor, she fell in love with photography. Not long after graduation, she opened her own studio back home in Maine, in Portland. She still operates it to this day. And she still loves photography. "It's my first passion," she states unhesitatingly.

Photography aside, Pat admits that she "always kind of wanted to own a bar." Toss in her and Trebor's newly-found appreciation of micro brewing and, voilà, it was not too terribly difficult to envision a brewpub. And that's precisely what the couple had in mind when they –

along with partners K.T. and Mike Snyder – purchased the former Dos Locos Restaurant in February of 1995 and re-named it the Hedgehog Brewpub... only to find out that, alas, opening a brewpub wasn't as easy as naming one. The partners ran into a wall of zoning problems, a wall so tall they finally decided they really didn't want to brew in Portland anyway.

Skowhegan to the rescue. Trebor also grew up in Skowhegan, where his dad, Skip, raised chickens. Until 1982. Since 1982 Skip's chicken barn has been sitting vacant. Pat and Trebor and K.T. and Mike decided that it should sit vacant no longer. That it had "brewery" written all over it. Christened the Oak Pond Brewing Company – after adjacent Oak Pond – Skowhegan's first brewery in 115 years is

scheduled to open the summer of 1996. Its main goal will be to supply the Hedgehog with some special brews. But Pat and partners plan to offer their wares in and around Skowhegan as well. After Portland and Skowhegan the sky could well be the limit. Whatever, Pat and the rest of the partners four – plus brewer Chris Morton – were all very definitely excited about Oak Pond/Hedgehog's future when I visited them in May 1996. "It's a really good industry and a really good group of people (in the industry)," is the way Pat summed things up.

OAK POND AT A GLANCE

If all goes as planned, Oak Pond's first brews will be introduced at the Hedgehog (q.v.) in Portland by late June 1996. Both ales and lagers are projected, with specific brand names as yet undecided. For directions and updated info call (207) 474-5952 (Oak Pond) or (207) 871-9124 (Hedgehog).

Photo, May 1996.
Pat, center, and associates Chris Morton, left, and Mike Snyder, right. Mike, who's 56, is (a) an Iowa native, (b) a research scientist, (c) an IDEXX, in Westbrook, employee (along with Trebor), and (d) a partner in Oak Pond/Hedgehog. He has a strong fondness for "well made beer;" respects quality over quantity. Chris, who's 25, is (a) a native of Portland, Maine who (b) relocated to Portland, Oregon for college (Lewis & Clark) and career (brewer at Full Sail Brewing Company) and then (c) relocated back to Maine for family roots and career (brewer at Oak Pond). He's eager to take part in Oak Pond's start-up and to see how his west coast brewing experience can, in his words, "complement the array of beers that already exist in Maine."

This entrance-to-the-brewery photo, taken in August 1995, does not do justice to the hugeness of Sea Dog's Bangor operation... which encompasses 24,000 square feet spread evenly over two floors. Admits Pete: "I had no idea how we were going to fill the entire building." But fill it he has... with the restaurant and actual brewing upstairs; conditioning, kegging, bottling, warehousing, and offices downstairs.

SEA DOG BREWING COMPANY
26 FRONT STREET, BANGOR 04401

He grew up in Buffalo but he wanted to be in Maine. That's the story of Pete Camplin, Sr. Born in New York's second largest city in 1943, Pete spent most of his childhood summers in Maine. Boothbay. Northport. Mostly Isleboro. "I can remember going to Maine when I was four," he smiles. It stuck with him. After high school, Pete chose to go to college in Maine (Colby, from which he graduated with a B.A. in 1965) and after college he chose to stay in Maine. But, alas, he wasn't able to. "There weren't," he explains, "a lot of employment opportunities around at the time." A job with a construction company in Washington, D.C. beckoned. Pete took it.

Pete and his wife Cindy - they were married in 1965 - liked Washington well enough. "Our heart, though, was in Maine," Pete makes perfectly clear. In 1971 he gambled and opened his own construction and development company in Kennebunk, later moving it to York Harbor. He and Cindy also dabbled in restaurants, owning eateries in York and Cape Neddick. All was fine except for one thing. Beer. Pete had grown up with good beer. "My dad was Canadian and he always had these 'strange' beers around,"

Pete laughs. Then there was the fraternity "brewery": Pete and roommate Russ Ives practiced the art of homebrewing all through their Colby days. "We used to lager our brew by hanging it out of the window on a rope," he laughs again. After college Pete kept his love of beer alive by sampling various and diverse imports. "I'd go out of my way to come up with the most exotic beers," he recalls.

Pete's route to full-fledged Maine brewer, though, probably would never have happened had it not been for a cross-country vacation Cindy and he took in 1991. They spent a fair chunk of time in Oregon and Washington. "That was my first exposure to brewpubs," states Pete. It was an exposure he liked. "I," he continues, "started to think it would really be something to combine the restaurant business with a little brewery… to be able to brew my own beer. And," to top it off, "to do it in Maine."

The first end result of Pete's thinking was the Sea Dog Brewing Company in Camden (q.v.), which opened in May 1993. The second end result is Sea Dog's brewery and restaurant in Bangor. Friends from Bangor kept suggesting a Sea Dog II. One went even further and mailed to Pete, in late 1993, an article on the City of Bangor's search for someone to develop a riverfront property they'd fallen heir to. Pete liked the thought of Bangor, looked at the property - a built-in-1949 former warehouse and former shoe factory - and was impressed with what he saw. "It was sort of cavernous for a restaurant but perfect for a brewery," he sums up.

Sixteen or so months later it *was* a brewery. And a full-scale restaurant, too. Opening day was March 8, 1995. In the ensuing months - I interviewed Pete in November 1995 - Pete's faith in Bangor has not diminished. Summer was far better than he'd ever dreamed. Fall was good, too. Pete's summation: "So far it's just been great."

SEA DOG / BANGOR AT A GLANCE
Sold first beer = 3/95. 1995 production = 8,000 barrels (85% bottled / 15% draught). Employees = 76 (incl. restaurant). Major brands = Sea Dog Old East India IPA, Sea Dog Windjammer Blonde Ale, Sea Dog Old Gollywobbler Brown Ale. Available from Maine south to Florida and west to Kentucky. For directions and tour/tasting info call (207) 947-8004.

Cindy and Pete enjoying themselves at the Maine Brewers' Festival, November 1995. One of the highlights of Sea Dog/Bangor happened the first month it was open. "There was," relays Pete, "an elderly gentleman who came in and who loved the beer and also the nautical antiques we have around the restaurant." He came a few times and then, one day, came again and told Pete he had something he'd like to show him. It was in the car, so Pete and the gentleman went outside. The gentleman opened his trunk and there was "this ancient bronze porthole." The gentleman said he'd like to donate it to the folks at the brewery. Pete accepted. And was touched. As he says: "It was an awfully nice welcoming to the community."

Photo, October 1995. The Sea Dog Brewing Company occupies part of two floors and part of the basement in the thoroughly-renovated four-story-plus-basement former Knox Woolen Mill, one block west of Route 1 in downtown Camden.

SEA DOG BREWING COMPANY
43 MECHANIC STREET, CAMDEN 04843

We wanted to "do a family business." So explains 30-year old Pete Camplin, Jr. when asked why he's in the brewing business. It made sense. Both Pete, Jr. and his dad, Pete, Sr., were longtime homebrewers; Pete, Jr.'s brother, Brett, had considerable experience as a chef; and Pete, Jr.'s wife, Karyn, had hotel management experience (as did Pete, Jr., himself). The idea of mustering all this background into brewing came together in January/February of 1990. Once the decision was made the big question, naturally enough, was where would the endeavor be. Pete, Jr. was born in New York state (Buffalo), raised in York Harbor, went to high school in New Hampshire, attended college in Orono. None of these places moved Pete, Jr. or the family. But Camden – where Pete, Sr. and his wife Cindy had been living since 1991 – was a different story. Camden moved them. The prospect of an oceanfront location especially moved them. But, alas, none was available. It was Pete, Sr. who spotted the brewery's eventual location… a 128-year old former woolen mill. "The place was a real mess," exclaims Pete, Jr…. but Pete, Sr. had a vision that transcended the mess. "He saw the waterfalls (Megunticook Falls, the former mill's source of power) and," recounts Pete, Jr., "said 'This is it!'"

Renovations to the mill began in August of 1992. They were not completed until the following spring. "It was a pretty tough rehab," laughs Pete, Jr. But well worth it, he's quick to add, noting that much of the work was done by the family. He's especially proud of the brewpub's booths... crafted by the father and son and son team of Pete, Sr., Pete, Jr., and Brett.

Sea Dog's grand opening took place May 15, 1993. To say it went well would be an understatement. "We were overwhelmed. The people packed the place," beams Pete, Jr. "We couldn't keep beer in the tanks or food in the kitchen." And when I interviewed Pete, Jr. in late October 1995 the people were still coming and Pete, Jr. was still beaming. "We have a lot of local support all-year around and then we have our traditional summer (translation = tourist) season," he told me.

Before we parted I asked Pete, Jr. how the name "Sea Dog" came about. You could tell he'd been asked the question before. "After my parents' Great Pyrenees," he replied, adding that the dog's given name is Barney, but that he likes to go sailing so much that Pete, Sr. and Cindy had taken to calling him "The Sea Dog."

One last question that I, of course, had to ask. "Which came first: 'Sea Dog,' the beer/brewery name or 'Sea Dogs,' the Portland baseball team name?" "We chose our name before they chose their name," is how Pete, Jr. fields that one. He's glad of the team's use of the name as well, though: "It adds to the (Sea Dog) name recognition: they (potential customers) have heard the name before."

SEA DOG / CAMDEN AT A GLANCE

Sold first beer = 5/93. 1995 production = 1,400 barrels (100% draught). Employees = 46 (incl. restaurant). Major brands = Sea Dog Old East India IPA, Sea Dog Windjammer Blonde Ale, Sea Dog Old Gollywobbler Brown Ale. Available throughout New England. For directions and tour/tasting info call (207) 236-6863.

Pete Camplin, Jr., October 1995. Pete, Jr., along with his wife Karyn, 26 (general management), and his brother Brett, 28 (chef), oversees the Camden side of the Sea Dog empire.

Photo, October 1995. Steve's brewery is located in a structure that sits behind his home. Fancy it is not. Formerly a cottage (i.e., community) hospital, Steve fashioned 800 square feet of the building into the Sheepscot Valley Brewing Company in 1994-1995. Steve admits the exterior is not likely to win too many beauty prizes, saying simply "Inside is more important than outside."

SHEEPSCOT VALLEY BREWING COMPANY
RR 1, BOX 88, WHITEFIELD 04353

"You need a lot of money to sell a lot of beer… but you don't need a lot of money to make a good beer." So stated Sheepscot Valley Brewing Company's Steve Gorrill when I spoke with him in October 1995. Asked if he'd read those words somewhere or if they were his slogan, Steve laughed and replied that neither was the case… that he'd just made them up as we talked. "But I might make it my slogan," he laughed again.

Steve is into beer because it fits his lifestyle. Born and raised in the Boston area, Steve's first stay in Maine came via Orono. He attended the University of Maine, graduating with a degree in animal science in 1985. That was also the year Steve began homebrewing. "Somebody gave me a homebrewing kit and I liked it because I was interested in different types of beers but didn't want to pay for them," laughs Steve yet again.

After college, Steve - and his wife Louisa, whom he'd met at Orono - went to Alaska a couple of times - "just to travel around" - before he settled down as a shellfish farmer, working at the Mook Sea Farm in Walpole, Maine. Working for someone else, though, wasn't what Steve wanted. "I wanted a kid and I wanted to be around to help raise him or her," he says flat out. The idea of turning home-brewing into businessbrewing came from a neighbor, David Chase. "He thought it would be great to have a local brewer." Steve agreed… and decided, in January of 1994, that he should be that brewer.

By late 1994 Steve and Louisa's Whitefield property was well on its way to becoming a brewery. Steve alternated between tinkering with equipment and business plans. It all came together in early 1995, with Steve's first commercial brew brightening his May. His first account - the Great Lost Bear in Portland - followed in early June.

Steve is the consummate small brewer. "I make it; I sell it; I deliver it," he says of his beer. Actually, "beers" would be more accurate: Steve takes considerable pride in the creation of new and somewhat wild and crazy brews. "Small brewers have to make something that's distinctive," he firmly believes. Mad Goose Ale (a Belgian-style ale named in honor of an uppity pet goose Steve once had) and Moondance (a Bavarian-style weiss beer named because Steve felt it would appeal to women) have been his flagship brews so far. But who's to know what's in the future? All Steve knows is that he's making a little money while having a lot of fun. And that he's doing it with the "help" of his son, one-year old Robert Louis Stephenson ("Rob") Gorrill. Steve and Rob. Rob and Steve. The Sheepscot Valley Brewing Company's Boys of Brewing.

SHEEPSCOT VALLEY AT A GLANCE
Sold first beer = 5/95. 1995 production = 65 barrels (100% draught). Employees = 1. Major brands = Mad Goose Ale, White Rabbit Wheat, Moondance Weiss, Lucifer's Hammer. Available at select locations in southern and mid-coast Maine. For directions and tour/tasting info call (207) 549-5530.

Steve in his brewhouse, October 1995. On his sales trips the 34-year old brewer often takes his infant son Rob with him. "He helps me sell," says Steve of his son. "If I take him into a bar with me people fawn over him… and then buy my beer."

Photo, October 1995. From metal fittings and wire rope to export ale and Blue Fin Stout: such is the story of the building that is home to Maine's largest brewery. Located at the base of Munjoy Hill, what is now the Shipyard Brewing Company was once the Crosby Laughlin foundry.

SHIPYARD BREWING COMPANY
86 NEWBURY STREET, PORTLAND 04101

"I was very successful. Then I was not so successful." That's how Fred Forsley sums up his career in real estate. It's the "not so successful" aspect that led to his becoming a Maine brewing mogul.

It all began when Fred was born, appropriately enough, in Portland in 1960. He was raised in Gray, returning to Portland to attend Cheverus High School. From there it was on to the University of New Hampshire. Real estate beckoned, however, and before long Fred was taking realty courses at USM and working for a Portland realtor as well as taking courses in Durham. He even attended Arizona State for a spell before graduating, from UNH, with a B.S. in 1983. His goal upon graduation: "To see if I could make a living selling real estate."

Anyone who lived in Maine in the 1980s knows the plot thereafter: first most everything went up; then most everything went down. By 1990 Fred was ready to make a career change.

Fortune smiled. An associate asked Fred to help him out of a losing venture in Kennebunk. The venture was called Harbor View Shops, a retail/restaurant complex with a high vacancy rate on Kennebunkport Harbor. Fred was able to negotiate the purchase of the property from the bank at a favorable price. What to do with it was something else. Fortune smiled once more. While visiting his brother Richard in Florida in late 1991, Fred was enjoying a brew in a local brewpub when he suddenly found himself saying - perhaps even shouting - "Hey, this would work in Kennebunk."

Back home Fred contacted Richard Pfeffer and Ed Stebbins of Gritty McDuff's. Would they be interested in operating a brewpub in Kennebunk? The answer, after some thought, came back "No." "But," they added, "we'll introduce you to (highly respected brewmaster) Alan Pugsley if you'd like to consider opening a brewpub of your own." The rest, as is often said, is history. Fred ordered his equipment in January 1992 and poured his first beer in June 1992. Alan oversaw the brewing while Fred, with help from silent partner Gordon Hurtubise, ran the sales and business side.

Jumping ahead to Portland (for more on Kennebunkport Brewing please see pages 140-141), Fred realized he'd outgrown Kennebunk as his sole brewing site by the summer of 1993. "We were pushing capacity in every direction: it was out of control," he sums up. Fred knew of a property that was available in Portland, the former Crosby Laughlin foundry at the base of Munjoy Hill. Part of the building went back to the early 1800s. Almost all of it, laughs Fred now, looked it. It was a mess. "Most people," he laughs again, "thought I was nuts." But Fred knew he wasn't nuts. He sealed the deal for the property in early December 1993.

When I interviewed Fred in January 1996 he was still upbeat. He smiles as he recalls the first day of brewing in Portland. He likens it to the feeling he had when his son Eli was born in early 1994. "This is the most emotional busi-

ness I can think of," he told me. "If people like your product you take it personally. If they don't you take it personally, too."

Emotion and business undoubtedly clashed in November 1995 when Fred agreed to become joint partners with America's second-largest brewing conglomerate, the Miller Brewing Company. "We (Shipyard) chose to do it because the industry is so capital intensive," Fred explains, adding: "It was either pull the brakes or give more fuel to the engine." With Miller money behind them, they'll be plenty of fuel in Shipyard's engine. Of equal importance: it is Shipyard personnel who will continue to control what does and doesn't go into Shipyard's beer. Brewmaster (and now co-partner) Alan Pugsley said it best when he said "If this (the partnership with Miller) compromises the integrity of the product, I'll be on the next plane back to England."

SHIPYARD AT A GLANCE
Sold first beer = 4/94. 1995 production = 30,500 barrels (70% bottled / 30% draught). Employees = 50. Major brands = Shipyard Export Ale, Goat Island Light, Blue Fin Stout, Old Thumper Ale. Available from Maine to Virginia plus Chicago. For directions and tour/tasting info call (207) 761-0807.

Photo, January 1996. Fred admits to being a far better beer salesman than beer brewer. "I'd be dangerous (at brewing)," he smiled and told me during my interview with him.

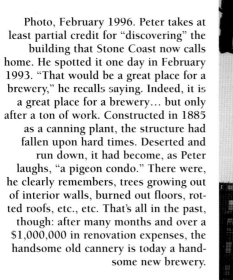

Photo, February 1996. Peter takes at least partial credit for "discovering" the building that Stone Coast now calls home. He spotted it one day in February 1993. "That would be a great place for a brewery," he recalls saying. Indeed, it is a great place for a brewery... but only after a ton of work. Constructed in 1885 as a canning plant, the structure had fallen upon hard times. Deserted and run down, it had become, as Peter laughs, "a pigeon condo." There were, he clearly remembers, trees growing out of interior walls, burned out floors, rotted roofs, etc., etc. That's all in the past, though: after many months and over a $1,000,000 in renovation expenses, the handsome old cannery is today a handsome new brewery.

STONE COAST BREWING COMPANY
YORK & CENTER STREETS, PORTLAND 04101

There must be something about the dryness of economics that leads people to the "wetness," if you will, of beer. Peter Camplin, Sr. of Sea Dog was an economics major. Richard Pfeffer of Gritty McDuff's was an economics major. Peter Leavitt of Sunday River/Stone Coast was an economics major (as was I, I must confess). And what was Peter's reaction to the world of economics and finance upon graduation (from Trinity, in 1987)? "I wanted to get as far away from it as possible," he answers without hesitation. That translated to California, where Peter's sister Joyce and her husband Greg lived. It was fortuitous: Greg was manager of the

Triple Rock Brewery, one of the Bay Area's pioneer brewpubs. Peter loved the place. "I hung out there a lot," he says. That was by night. By day he did a little of this and a little of that. Some cooking. Some catering. Some construction. It was good money. "But I couldn't see myself doing any of it ten years down the road," he notes. That changed in mid-1988. While at Triple Rock one evening one of the brewpub's brewers told Peter he was looking for help. "Are you interested?," he asked. The pay was lousy... but the appeal (of making beer) was there. Peter talked with his mother. She encouraged him to go for it. "It'll be an education as well as a job," she told him. Peter started at Triple Rock in August of 1988. Almost immediately he knew brewing was what he wanted to do. "I *can* see myself doing this in ten years," he said to himself.

Peter stayed at Triple Rock for two years, leaving in 1990 to help start-up a new brewpub. All went well with the new venture - the Twenty Tank Brewery, also in San Francisco - until Peter realized he'd had it with California. He missed the east (he was born in Maryland; grew up in Massachusetts) and its change of seasons and its relative lack of people. First, though, came a ten-week brewing course at the highly respected Siebel Institute in Chicago, followed by a stint as a consultant to Telluride Brewing in Colorado.

In April 1992 Peter met Grant Wilson at a micro-brewers' convention. Grant was in the thinking-about-opening-a-brewery phase of Sunday River (q.v.). He and Peter talked. Several months later Grant and Peter talked again. "I need someone (with brewing and

start-up experience) right away," said Grant. "Okay," said Peter.

When I spoke with Peter three and a half years later, in March 1996, he was delighted with his career path. After helping Sunday River come to fruition he and Grant tackled Portland. "We saw a lot of good beer being drunk there (Portland) and there was only one brewpub," Peter explained, adding "We felt there was definitely room for more than that." Opened in late January 1996, Stone Coast has been all that Peter could have wanted so far. "We have a great team working here," he states. Business has been good. More importantly, Peter's very pleased with the prospect of everything being fully in place for summer... when those seasonal hoards called tourists will, hopefully, once again descend upon Maine.

STONE COAST AT A GLANCE
Sold first beer = 1/96. 1995 production = 0 barrels. Employees = 60 (incl. restaurant). Major brands = 420 IPA, Stone Coast Stout, Cannery Kolsch, 5 Points ESP. Available only at Stone Coast. For directions and tour/tasting info call (207) 773-BEER.

Photo, March, 1996. When I asked Peter, who's 31 and who oversees the brewing at both Sunday River and Stone Coast, how the name Stone Coast came to be he replied that there was a desire to select a name that was "evocative of Maine's rocky coast." Grant came up with "Stone Coast" and it seemed to fit the bill. So Stone Coast it is.

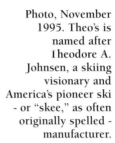

Photo, November 1995. Theo's is named after Theodore A. Johnsen, a skiing visionary and America's pioneer ski - or "skee," as often originally spelled - manufacturer.

SUGARLOAF BREWING COMPANY/THEO'S RESTAURANT & BREWPUB
SUGARLOAF/USA ACCESS ROAD / RR 1, BOX 2268, CARRABASSET VALLEY 04947

When I asked Dick Leeman and Jim McManus, co-proprietors of Sugarloaf Brewing and Theo's Restaurant & Brewpub, if they could think of a heartwarming story, they beamed. And told me of *The Case Of The Disappearing Bar.* It seems Dick and Jim purchased a 25-foot bar before they were ready to set it in place at Theo's. Result = storage. The duo dutifully loaded the bar into a truck and set off, "so happy and so proud," for their storage facility. When they arrived and went to unload their new posseson, however, it was gone. "Where's the bar?" they asked of each other. Fate was on their side, though: retracing their route, Dick and Jim found the bar - all 25 feet of it - just sitting

in the middle of the road. Case solved. It now resides in the brewpub's game room.

Surprising as it may sound, Dick and Jim did not have a lifelong desire to be carting - and losing - bars. Dick, who was born in Colorado in 1955 but lived in Bangor from age one on, and Jim, also born in 1955 and the pride of East Winthrop, had other plans in mind. After graduation from USM, Dick's desires revolved around urban planning. Jim attended UMO for three years and then "retired" to form a company that consults nursing homes on fire safety.

Slowly but surely, though, Dick and Jim pursued paths that led to Carrabasset Valley. Dick forsook urban planning for food service, working his way from dishwasher to kitchen manager. He also learned to bartend, a skill he practiced at the Seamen's Club in Portland for five years. Later restaurant experience included Jamison's Tavern in Freeport and Channel Crossing in South Portland. Friend Jim, meanwhile, was becoming intrigued with the idea of making beer. He'd been a homebrewer since his UMO days, but carried it one big step further when, in 1993, he took a brewing course at Kennebunkport Brewing in Kennebunk. He kept Dick posted on his progress. And his excitement. "He," laughs Dick, "said 'Wouldn't it be fun (to be brewers)?'"

The two got serious in late 1993. They began to scout possible locations. They looked at Bangor. And Portland. And Waterville. And Augusta. And discarded them all in favor of Carrabasset Valley and Sugarloaf / USA. There they purchased

a 25-year old building that had been a Ski Rack Shop. They liked the notion that they could focus on-premise - both food and drink - from December to April and off-premise - via bottled brew - the remainder of the year. "It promised a steady cash flow all year long," Dick explains.

Since their opening in late June 1994, Dick and Jim have been amazed at the public's response. The more they brew, it seems, the more people want. "We can't," stated Jim when I visited Carrabasset Valley in November 1995, "keep up with the demand." But Jim's not complaining. "I think it's fantastic," he says. Adds Dick: "We're having a great time."

SUGARLOAF AT A GLANCE
Sold first beer = 7/94. 1995 production = 2,310 barrels (75% bottled / 25% draught). Employees = 40 (incl. restaurant). Major brands = Carrabassett IPA, Carrabassett Pale Ale, Carrabassett Kolsch, Amos Winter Ale. Available throughout Maine. For directions and tour/tasting info call (207) 237-2211.

Photo, November 1995, showing Dick, left, and Jim, right. That's brewmaster Jeff Hinckley in the middle. Jeff, who graduated from UMO with a degree in electrical engineering technology, began his career in beer when he opened a homebrew supply store in his home town of Winthrop in 1992. From there he turned to creating home-brews himself. He joined Sugarloaf in May of 1994 and has crafted the brewery's many brews - including "Misery Ale" - since. What's Misery Ale? Well, it was the brewery's first commercial brew and, reminisces Jeff, named in honor of all the aggrivation and red tape involved in the brewery's startup.

Photo, August 1995. The brewery's exterior was designed by the Portland architectural firm of Goduti-Thomas, while the brewery itself (i.e., that part of the building where the beer is actually made) was designed by Sunday River's brewmaster, Peter Leavitt. "We wanted it (the brewery) to be the focal point... to be smack in the middle of the building," states Grant. It is.

SUNDAY RIVER BREWING COMPANY
ROUTE 2 & SUNDAY RIVER ROAD, P.O. BOX 824, BETHEL 04217

Out of the mouths of grandmothers comes wisdom. Just ask Grant Wilson. He knows. It was late 1991. Grant had moved back to his native Massachusetts following three years of college in Santa Cruz, California. While in California he had become intrigued with the multitude of micros and brewpubs. His every intention was to open, in partnership with his cousin, Hans Trupp, a similar venture in the Bay State. But Hans and he, both then 23, were getting nowhere. "We couldn't find a location we wanted at a budget we could afford," Grant phrases it.

Enter grandma. Grant was having dinner with his grandmother, Eleanor, in Lexington, Massachusetts in November. She'd retired to Maine. To Bryant Pond. After hearing Grant's looking-for-the-right-site woes she said "You really ought to think about putting your brewery in Bethel." Grant still laughs. "I thought she was crazy," he says. After several more months of site-selection blues, however, Grant and Hans began to think maybe Eleanor wasn't so crazy after all. In February of 1992 they took a trip to Bethel and started to poke around. While looking at a site that *was* for sale they discovered their dream location... a cornfield on Route 2, three miles east of downtown Bethel, that *wasn't* for sale. Grant yet vividly recalls that Hans and he looked at each other and said, almost in unison, "That's the spot to be." In March they made an offer. It was accepted... and they were off and running. Construction began in June and was finished, per Grant, "on the 19th of December." The brewpub had opened on the 18th.

When I interviewed Grant in November of 1995 he was pleased. Work was progressing nicely on Hans' and his Stone Coast Brewing facility (q.v.) in Portland; Sunday River's beer and food service was where he wanted it to be ("We went through a couple of chefs in the first few months," he recounts); and he'd just begun

to bottle a portion of the brewery's output. "But," he assured me, "we're not going to be doing much bottled volume: we're a brewpub. That's what we want to concentrate on."

And Grant's grandmother, Eleanor: how does she feel about the way things have turned out? "Oh, she comes in and she likes the beer," says Grant. "But," he admits, "she prefers Scotch."

SUNDAY RIVER AT A GLANCE
Sold first beer = 1/93. 1995 production = 2750 barrels (98% draught / 2% bottled). Employees = 45 (incl. restaurant). Major brands = Redstone Ale, Black Bear Porter, Sunday River Alt, Baron's Brown Ale. Available at select locations in southern and central Maine. For directions and tour/tasting info call (207) 824-4ALE.

Photo, November 1995. I inquired of Grant if he'd yet named a beer in honor of his grandmother, Eleanor. He smiled and said "no." But he has named one - Tinker's Ale - in honor of his grandfather, whose nickname was "Tinker." Asked if he thought his grandfather would approve, Grant smiled again and said "I think he wouldn't mind."

Karen Geary offers up a Geary's at the 1994 Festival...

...while Julie Pepi does likewise with an Allagash White at the 1995 extravaganza.

THE MAINE BREWERS' FESTIVAL

If you're really into brew the highlight of your entire calendar year could well be the first Saturday in November. That's the day that each and every Maine brewer journeys to Portland and shares their wares with thousands of beer aficionados. It's called the Maine Brewers' Festival and it's held at the Exposition Building ("The Expo"), located at 236 Park Avenue. There are two shows, one from 1:30 to 5:30 and one from 7:00 to 11:00. There's food and live music. But mostly there's beer. And you never...

THE GREAT STATE OF MAINE BEER BOOK's roving reporter was on hand for both the 1994 and 1995 editions of the Maine Brewers' Festival. In 1995 he asked a random sampling of attendees why they were attending. Here is what they said.

Mark Lindberg, Standish: "Beer. I love beer!"

Dawn Devine and Dan Paradis, Portland: "To sample the best beer in Maine."

Greg Bowden, Biddeford; Jennifer Leonard, Biddeford; Troy LaPlante, Van Buren: "The great beers."

Al Diamon, Portland: "This is the only chance all year to try all of Maine's beers at one place."

Amanda Cottrell, Amherst, Mass.: "We make our own beer at home and we wanted to see what the micros were up to."

Jane and Doug Doherty, Biddeford: "The great brew and the wide variety."

Craig McNeal, West Kennebunk, and Michael Perry, Portland: "We brew our own beer and we came to compare."

Mike and Leigh Raposo, Standish: "To check out all the beer and to do a little Christmas shopping for tee-shirts (Leigh)." "To try all the Maine beers. Instead of driving hundreds of miles we can come here and try them all at once (Mike)."

...can tell who might show up. Here's Governor Angus King smiling for my camera at the 1995 shindig. Asked his favorite beer, the Gov replied: "I may be brave but I'm not stupid (to choose one brew... and risk offending fans of all the others!)."

Vacationland's Very Best: The Best Bets For Maine-Brewed Brews

Photo, February 1996.
Catherine "on the job" at the
Great Lost Bear

Here they are: the **TOP TWENTY** bars, restaurants and other pleasure spas in Maine in terms of the number of Maine-brewed beers on draught! This has been no easy assignment. But with considerable help from chambers of commerce, beer distributors, brewers, beer buffs, and the bars and restaurants themselves we've done it. I say "we" because my wife Catherine has been very much a part of this section of THE GREAT STATE OF MAINE BEER BOOK.

Here's what we did. First, we tracked down every lead we could... and ended up talking with – via telephone – close to 100 hopefuls. Then it was "field research time": we visited each and every candidate with substantial Maine brews on tap. For each establishment we applied a simple two-part formula: one point for each different Maine brew on draught and one additional point for each different Maine brewery represented. Example: ten Maine beers / eight Maine breweries = 18. Pretty simple. Very effective. Over the next seven pages we're proud to present the grand winners (plus the tops in take-out establishments, too) with the total point score for each in parentheses. **THE TOP TWENTY.** Congratulations!

N.B. It goes without saying that a brewpub is the very best place to enjoy a beer. That's where it's the freshest. However, a number of Maine's brewpubs – Bear Brewpub (Orono), Bray's (Naples), Federal Jack's (Kennebunk), Great Falls (Auburn), Gritty McDuff's (Freeport), Maine Coast (Bar Harbor), Narrow Gauge (Farmington), Stone Coast (Portland), Sunday River (Bethel), and Theo's (Carrabasset Valley) – did not make our list of THE TOP TWENTY. That's because they, understandably, feature their own brews and so score low re the "breweries rep-resented" factor. High point score or not, these are places not to be missed!

1-THE GREAT LOST BEAR, 540 FOREST AVENUE, PORTLAND (50)

When you walk into the Great Lost Bear you walk into a beerlovers' paradise. "When people come in," exclaims co-owner Dave Evans, "they're bedazzled. They gawk." He laughs: "And then we tell them there's more (taps) around the corner."

But it wasn't always so. Proprietors Dave, his wife Weslie, and cousin and lifelong friend Douglas "Chip" MacConnell, Jr., easily recall their very early days at the Bear. "We bought what had been a rock club called 'Bottoms Up' on June 1, 1979," reminisces Dave. "It was tattered," reminisces Chip. Eighteen days and nights later ("We'd put in 18-hour days and sleep on the floor and every three days go home and take a shower": Dave) they opened as the Grizzly Bear. At first, though, they were "partners" with a bakery. Explains Chip: "We shared the building with Nappi's Bakery and every night about 9:00 they'd fire up their ovens and there'd be this cloud of misty yeast hovering in the air." Chuckles Dave: "We lost a lot of customers." "But," bounces back Chip, "the bread (delivery) was always prompt!"

By 1981 the Grizzly Bear's fame had spread to the west coast. But not in the way that Dave and Weslie and Chip had envisioned. They heard from a chain called Grizzly Bear Pizza in Oregon… and were told to cease and desist with the Grizzly Bear name. It seems they – the pizza people – had trademarked it. The Great Lost Bear became the enterprise's new name. The reason: "Bear" was in it and it started with a "G."

The Bear was basically your average bar its first seven years of being. Bud in bottles. Genesee and Stroh's and Miller Lite on tap. Then, in late 1986, David Geary came

The sign painted on the outside of the Great Lost Bear says it all: there is, very simply, no place like it when it comes to Maine beer in Maine. It is Number One.

calling: "Would you be interested in carrying a beer I'm brewing right here in Portland?" The answer was an immediate "Yes." "We liked the idea of supporting a local business," states Chip.

Ten years later the Great Lost Bear is still supporting local business. Only now "local" translates to Lincolnville and Liberty and Bar Harbor and beyond. On draught at the Bear is an astounding 36 Maine brews representing an equally astounding 14 Maine breweries (Allagash, Andrew's, Atlantic, Casco Bay, Geary's, Great Falls, Gritty's, Lake St. George, Maine Coast, Sea Dog, Sheepscot Valley, Shipyard, Sugarloaf, Sunday River). No one need fear going thirsty at the Great Lost Bear.

Part of the GLB's allure is its decor. Described by Dave as "funky," by Weslie as "eclectic," and by Chip as "grandma's attic," it's more or less wall-to-wall old ads and photos and pennants and posters. Says Dave: "There's something here for everyone."

Photo, February 1996. Left to right: Chip, Weslie, Dave. From the Garden State to the Pine Tree State: all three of the Bear's partners were born and raised in New Jersey. Do they miss the old home state? "Not at all," says Dave. "Maine is our home."

Entrance, March 1996

PLEASE NOTE: ON MAY 1, 1996 ED NOYES ANNOUNCED THE CLOSING OF MORGAN-FIELD'S FOR FINANCIAL AND PERSONAL REASONS. AS OF PRESS-TIME HE WAS STILL HOPING, HOWEVER, TO RE-OPEN. BOTH BLUES AND BEER FANS HOPE THAT HE WILL.

2- MORGANFIELD'S, 121 CENTER STREET, PORTLAND (39)

Before he opened his blues club, Morganfield's, Ed Noyes conducted a survey. He asked area blues fans what features they'd like to see in such a venture. The answers: a good sound system, good sightlines, no smoking… and a good choice of good beers. Ed has obliged all the way around. The sound is great, there's nary a bad seat in the house, smoking is limited, and Morganfield's beer menu is sure to brighten even the bluest of the blue. There's a whopping 26 Maine brews on draught, representing a mighty impressive 13 Maine breweries (Allagash, Andrew's, Atlantic, Casco Bay, Geary's, Great Falls, Lake St. George, Maine Coast, Sea Dog, Sheepscot Valley, Shipyard, Sugarloaf, Sunday River). There's also a solid 75 different beers by the bottle.

Of course, Morganfield's is more than just a beerlovers' haven. Opened in June of 1994, it features live music most every night of the week. Blues, naturally, is the mainstay, but Ed books Cajun, R&B, and some rock 'n roll as well.

Still, though, it's the beers that interest us. Bar manager Jeff Sailor says people get a kick out of the selection. "They like to be dazzled," he puts it. Jeff is dazzled, too. He admits to getting great joy out of trying all the new micro brands and varieties. "Now I'm a married man with a wife and kids," he laughs. "Whereas I used to go for parties and women, now my passion is beer." Jeff's favorite? "I like 'em all," he says upon reflection.

3- TAPS TAVERN, 446 FORE STREET, PORTLAND, (26)

When Taps opened in Three Dollar Dewey's old location in August of 1995 it devoted a lot of its lines to "from away" micro brews. West coast stuff. It was a mistake. But it was a mistake rectified when P.J. Lewis took over as manager in September. "People would come in and want Maine beers," P.J. told us when we talked with her in February 1996. "Especially the tourists," she added. "They want to know what's made right here (in Maine)." Well, what's made in Maine is now what P.J. offers. Taps features 18 Maine brews on draught, representing eight Maine breweries (Allagash, Andrew's, Atlantic, Casco Bay, Geary's, Sea Dog, Shipyard, Sugarloaf). Decor is darts, billiards, and a king-sized picnic table gathered around an attractive brick-encased bar. Menu is sandwiches, soups, salads, and nachos / wings.

P.S. The Baker's Table, several doors down (at 434 Fore) and under the same management as Taps, also has a heady Maine-beer-on-tap selection.

Exterior sign, February 1996

4- JOSHUA'S TAVERN, 121A MAINE ST., BRUNSWICK (23)

When it opened in 1990 Joshua's had two beers on tap. You can probably guess what they were. (Hint: one began with a "B"; the other with an "M."). It's six years later and Joshua's – named after Maine's favorite Civil War general – now has 21 beers on tap, with 15 of them from Maine. Eight (Allagash, Casco Bay, Geary's, Lake St. George, Sea Dog, Shipyard, Sugarloaf, Sunday River) Maine breweries are represented. Twenty-nine year old co-proprietor and manager T.J. Siatras told us he was just keeping up with "the rhythm" of the bar industry. "That (a lot of beers) is what people are looking for," he explained. "They are adventure seekers. They like to try different things." They're certainly trying what T.J. is offering: he reports that his draught beer sales, which used to account for about 30-40% of his total beer sales, now account for about 80-90%!

Exterior sign, April 1996

Decor could be called hodge-podge: college pennants, antique sports gear, old signs, and our favorite, a shoe store shoe-sizer. Actually, T.J. described it best when he said "The taps themselves are my decor." Menu off-season is lighter fare (appetizers, sandwiches, four dinner entrées), with summer – and an outside deck – much more extensive.

5- THREE DOLLAR DEWEY'S, 241 COMMERCIAL STREET, PORTLAND (22)

Founded in 1981, Three Dollar Dewey's is Maine's pioneer "beer bar." First to pour Bass on tap. First to pour Guinness on tap. First to use pint glasses. The list of firsts is long. And general manager Donn Berry is proud of every one of them. "Up to six years ago," he told us, "we had to beg for product. The distributors wanted to dabble with the micros rather than run with them. Now," he laughs, "they're grabbin' 'em up as best they can."

Originally located where Taps is now, Dewey's has been enjoying its new location since July 1995. On the ground floor of the handsome red brick 1851 Hersey Block, the new Dewey's yet features an English-style pub atmosphere… only now it's larger-in-size English-style pub atmosphere. With a lot of brick and dark green. The centerpiece is the bar, which touts 14 Maine brews on draught representing eight Maine brewers (Allagash, Andrew's, Atlantic, Geary's, Sea Dog, Sheepscot Valley, Shipyard, Sugarloaf). Menu is traditional bar: burgers, salads, sandwiches, pizza, plus specials and Dewey's Famous 3-Alarm Chili.

Coaster, February 1996. Legend has it that in gold rush / "bawdy house" days a man who wanted female companionship got what he paid for. For $1.00 he got "lookie." For $2.00 he got "feelie." For $3.00 he got "dooie." For $3.00 nowadays he (or she) gets "pintee."

6- THE HEDGEHOG PUB, 35 INDIA STREET, PORTLAND (21)

What began life as the Hedgehog Brewpub is now the Hedgehog ~~Brew~~ Pub. That's because, explains co-proprietor Trebor Lawton, "There were so many regulations we would have had to basically reconstruct the building (to make it into a brewpub)." Instead Trebor and associates are going off-site via a brewery in Skowhegan (see Oak Pond Brewing). When we visited in April, however, Oak Pond was in the future… but the present wasn't bad. There were an even dozen Maine brews on tap, representing nine Maine breweries (Allagash, Andrew's, Atlantic, Casco Bay, Geary's, Great Falls, Lake St. George, Sea Dog, Shipyard). Even when Oak Pond is up and about, Trebor assured us, there'll be a healthy choice of "guest" brews on tap. Also featured: a most attractive cherry bar and what Trebor feels is "the best beer garden in town." A pool table, darts, sizable dance floor (there's live music three or so nights a week) and a snappy burgundy, green and white color scheme rounds things out. Menu is salads, sandwiches and basic bar plus a selection of seven pasta dishes, all heavily endowed with garlic. During the summer months there's a lot more emphasis on seafood.

Logo, 1996. A hedgehog is more or less an English porcupine. Why name your pub after one? "Because," answers Trebor, "It's distinctive. It's fun. People remember it."

7- THE FORGE, 42 WHARF STREET, PORTLAND (19)

When we visited The Forge it was February and things were on the quiet side. But you could tell that come "the season" it's a place to be. There are two floors plus, for summertime fun, an outdoor patio. Built into a circa 1820 brick building that once was actually a forge, The Forge is rich in brick and various woods. Manager Bruce Mann is justifiably proud that he constructed the bar – himself – out of wood he rescued when the Lewiston Raceway was torn down.

The Forge has featured Maine brews since Bruce and his wife Rebecca opened in 1994. On tap the day of our visit were 12 Maine beers representing seven Maine breweries (Allagash, Atlantic, Casco Bay, Geary's, Sea Dog, Shipyard, Sunday River). "I think people appreciate the difference," Bruce says of his customers' preference for Vacationland brews. Food at The Forge is ordered-in from next-door T.O.N.Y. Baloney (brick oven pizza / wedges / salads).

Exterior sign, Feb. 1996

8 (TIE)- BLEACHERS SPORTS BAR & RESTAURANT, 334 FOREST AVE., PORTLAND (17)

Twenty-five year old Chris Pillsbury has been manager of Bleachers for two years. He's been a good influence. "My goal," he says, "has been to get some of those Bud drinkers to expand their horizons." To try some of the Maine brews he's put in. So far Chris, who's a homebrewing enthusiast and who admits to a fondness for good beer himself, is pleased with his progress. He will say, though, that Bleachers still draws what he calls "a pale ale crowd." "I've tried brown ales and porters and they haven't done well," he told us. Nevertheless, Bleachers had a formidable array of brews on its line-up card the day Catherine and I stopped in, in February. There were nine Maine beers on draught representing eight Maine breweries (Allagash, Andrew's, Atlantic, Casco Bay, Geary's, Shipyard, Sugarloaf, Sunday River).

Exterior sign, Feb. 1996

Sports photos and memorabilia line the walls. That's not surprising: Bleachers is, after all, a sports bar. A lot of it is baseball. And that's good! (Can you spot Pee Wee Reese? Or Jimmy "Double X" Foxx? They're there.). There are also seven TV screens. Menu is basic bar: burgers, wings, salads, sandwiches.

Top Of The Take-Out Heap…

Maine doesn't have beer and booze "supermarkets" such as can be found in Massachusetts and Maryland and some other states, but we are certainly not deprived with respect to "beer to go," either. Here's a **Top Three**… with a Next-Best-Top 21. It is based on input from brewers, distributors, chambers of commerce, and the stores and markets themselves.

Here's a quickie quiz for you. What does "RSVP" stand for? If your answer is "Répondez s'il vous plait" (Respond, if you please) you'd be correct. Most of the time. But when it comes to **RSVP DISCOUNT BEVERAGE** (874 Forest Avenue, **Portland** and 894 Main Street, **Westbrook**) it stands for "Redemption/Service/Variety/Price." That's per Peter Welch who, along with partners Peter Cleveland and Rick Shappy, owns RSVP. "We weighed a lot of names before we chose that one," states Peter. "And we use those four words to help us make decisions."

RSVP's Portland facility opened in 1981; Westbrook, in 1985. Both feature most impressive beer selections. I asked Peter if he thought RSVP has the largest beer selection in the state. His response: "Everybody tells us we do." He quickly adds "We work very hard at it."

Both personally and professionally Peter, who's 40, is delighted with the micro "revolution" in Maine. "It's fun," he says before turning philosophical: "I think the public has a sense of yearning for something they can touch and feel and call their own; a search for identity in a world where we're losing that." Micro-brewed beers, sums up Peter, serve that purpose. "You may know the brewer or his/her family or one of the employees." It's a point and a good one and it leads to only one conclusion: whether you're searching for beer or searching for identity, RSVP is a marvelous place to do the searching.

Photo, RSVP/Portland, January 1996

My vote for best take-out number two goes to an emporium in the New Auburn section of **Auburn**. It's **FLORIAN'S MARKET** (286 Main Street) and it's a beerlovers' mecca. In operation since 1963, Florian's began to put an emphasis on out-of-the-ordinary beers in the early 1980s. "We just wanted to have something different than everybody else had," explains Florian's proprietor, 48-year-old Auburn native Florian "Junior" Magno.

At first that "something different" translated to imported brews. Then came the micros from elsewhere. *Then* came the micros from Maine. Florian's now features what it bills its "Massive 30-Door Cooler." And they do, indeed, have 30 cooler doors wrapped around the store. I know because I counted them! More impressive: 19 of the 30 are reserved for beer. If it's a Maine beer, Florian's either has it or will get it. Junior sees to that. He tells of the times he'd meet Suzi Foster of Bar Harbor Brewing midway between Bar Harbor and Auburn. In a parking lot in Newport. "We'd load beer off her truck and onto mine," he laughs. Junior, ironically, is not exactly a big beer buff himself. "I can drink a beer if I have to, but that's it," he says, adding "but I have knowledgeable customers who keep me informed as to what is what." Florian's definitely reflects what is what.

Photo, Florian's, January 1996

Photo, Jokas', February 1996

...Plus Some Of The Best Among All The Rest

Alternative Market, 99 Main St., Bar Harbor

The Bag & Bottle, Route 2 East, Bethel

Belfast Co-op Store, 69 High Street, Belfast

The Bottle Shop, off Route 1, Wells

Broadway Redemption Center, 771 Broadway, South Portland

Burby & Bates Beverage Warehouse, 7 Oak Street, Orono

Coastal Discount Beverage, 559 Elm St., Route 1, Biddeford

Farm Town Market, Route 4 North, Farmington

Good Food Store, Route 2 East, Bethel

Hope General Store, Hope

John Edward's Whole Foods Market, 158 Main Street, Ellsworth

Lily, Lupine & Fern Emporium, 37-39 Bayview St., Camden

Lou's Beverage Barn, 75 Bangor Street, Augusta

MicroSpirits, 213 Ohio Street, Bangor

Natural Living Center, 421 Wilson Street, Brewer

Oak Hill Discount Beverage, 26 Oak Hill Plaza, Scarborough

Quality Market, 145 College Avenue, Lewiston

C.E. Reilly & Son, Route 130, New Harbor

The Store/Ampersand, 22 Mill Street, Orono

Tess' Market, 54½ Pleasant Street, Brunswick

Tiger Town Beverage, 40 Maine Avenue, Gardiner

Rounding out my choice for the Top Three Take-Out is **JOKAS' DISCOUNT BEVERAGE** in **Waterville** (52 Front Street). Jokas' has been owned and operated by 45-year old Waterville native Joe Karter and his brother Fred since 1987. From the beginning they've been big on lesser-known beers. "It was something we discussed," says Joe. They noticed nobody else was carrying much of anything very exotic... so they decided they would. In those early days, Joe laughs, they had 11 cooler doors and everything fit nicely. Now Jokas' has 23 doors and they're straining at the gills to do justice to all the brands and varieties they stock. Joe, however, isn't complaining. He's delighted at what he sees. "There's a whole new generation of beer drinkers," he notes, "and they're willing to pay more because it – micro-brewed beer – tastes good." Adds Joe: "I don't have a slow (moving) Maine beer."

Exterior sign, Burby & Bates, Orono

Interior sign, The Bag & Bottle, Bethel

Window sign, MicroSpirits, Bangor

8 (TIE)- LOMPOC CAFE & BREWPUB, 36 RODRICK STREET, BAR HARBOR (17)

Exterior sign, May 1996

Forget beer and baseball. At the Lompoc it's beer and bocce. You can sip a little and bowl a little on proprietor Doug Maffucci's pride and joy, the only open-to-the-public bocce court on Mount Desert Island. Or you can just enjoy the beer: Doug features six of his own Atlantic Brewing (q.v.) brews on tap as well as draught choices from five other Maine micros (Geary's, Gritty's, Shipyard, Sugarloaf, and one rotating). Says Doug: "We're perfectly happy to sell other people's beer as well as our own." Open from mid-May to mid-November, the Lompoc offers food choices from soup and salads to peanut chicken and shrimp etouffe with homemade pita-crust pizza in between.

8 (TIE)- THE SUDS PUB, LOWER MAIN STREET, BETHEL (17)

Menu Design, Jan. 1996

Located within the quite magnificent built-in-1873 Sudbury Inn, Suds offers 10 Maine brews representing seven Maine breweries (Andrew's, Geary's, Lake St. George, Sea Dog, Shipyard, Sugarloaf, Sunday River). "We do a lot of beer," waiter / front desk man / all-around employee Nigel Serbe told us. "A fair amount of bottles… but primarily draught." And most of it is Maine draught. "People visiting," acknowledged Nigel, "want to try Maine beers."

Decor-wise, Catherine noticed the checkered tablecloths, slanted wood paneling, and the unique-to-us wraparound wooden bench. I noticed the old advertising, especially the wonderful Hotel Sudbury ("Rooms $2.50 up") sign. Menu is eclectic bar.

The Suds Pub is open daily from 4:00/5:00 PM to 1:00 AM year 'round except for a three-week period in May that Nigel described as "late mud season." Live entertainment is featured Thursday through Saturday.

12- RUPUNUNI, 119 MAIN STREET, BAR HARBOR (15)

Logo, May 1996

Rupununi could be characterized as an American cafe with a strong South American flavor. Spread over two very sizable floors, it takes its name from a river in British Guyana that proprietor Michael Boland studied as part of his college thesis work. It's a bar/restaurant that has it all: outdoor patio, upstairs veranda ("Carmen Veranda"), a pair of pool tables, live music and dancing three nights a week… and plenty of beer choices. On tap are eight Maine brews representing seven Maine breweries (Allagash, Atlantic, Casco Bay, Geary's, Maine Coast, Sea Dog, Shipyard). Open from late April until January, Rupununi features a complete menu, ranging from salads and burgers to lobster, buffalo, and venison.

13 (TIE)- THE SAMOSET, WARRINGTON ST., ROCKPORT (14)

Take a 150-room resort complete with an 18-hole golf course, putting green, tennis, fitness trails, etc. and blend in a bar that serves seven Maine beers representing seven Maine breweries (Andrew's, Geary's, Lake St. George, Sea Dog, Shipyard, Sugarloaf, Sunday River) and you have the Samoset. The bar area, called the Breakwater Lounge, serves casual food, while next-door Marcel's serves complete meals. The view of Penobscot Bay from both is quite marvelous.

13 (TIE)- SEAMEN'S CLUB RESTAURANT, 1 EXCHANGE ST., PORTLAND (14)

The Seamen's Club occupies two floors of the landmark – built in 1866-1867 – Charles Q. Clapp Block in the Old Port Exchange. Upstairs there are three dining rooms; downstairs there's additional dining space and the bar. Featured are eight Maine beers on draught, representing six Maine breweries (Atlantic, Geary's, Sea Dog, Shipyard, Sugarloaf, Sunday River). The best seller? "It's Geary's Hampshire Ale. Hands down," bar manager Jason McPhee, 27, told us, adding "During the winter months when it's available I can't keep it in stock." The Seamen's decor is gracious upstairs; less gracious downstairs. Menu is full-scale restaurant with an emphasis on, not surprisingly, seafood.

15-DENNETT'S WHARF, SEA STREET, CASTINE (13)

Catherine describes Dennett's Wharf as possessing "a large lobster shack look." And that's good. Then there's the deck. And that's very good. In fact, the deck at Dennett's Wharf is one of the more scenic spots in Maine to enjoy a brew or two: you're so close to the Bagaduce River you almost feel you're in it. Dennett's Wharf, open from May until October, is more than just scenery, though. There's beer. Proprietor Gary Brouillard features seven Maine beers on draught, representing six Maine micros (Andrew's, Atlantic, Casco Bay, Geary's, Shipyard, Sugarloaf). And food. Choices run the gamut from sandwiches and salads to full-course dinners, with seafood the specialty.

Exterior sign, May 1996

Neon Sign,
February 1996

16 (TIE)- SHELLEY'S, 12 LINCOLN STREET, BIDDEFORD (12)

"People were telling me they had to drive into Portland to get any micro beers," Shelley Pelletier told us when we visited Shelley's in February. So Shelley, 35, decided to rectify that situation: she started to carry micros in her place. That was 1994. Two years later she's up to seven Maine brews on tap representing five Maine brewers (Atlantic, Casco Bay, Gritty's, Shipyard, Sugarloaf).

Housed in the huge – 6,000 or so square feet – first floor of a former Pepperell Mill building, Shelley's also features pool (11 tables) and live rock & roll bands (Tuesday, Friday, Saturday nights). Food selection is pizza.

16 (TIE)- SEA DOG BREWPUB, 26 FRONT ST., BANGOR (12)

As with its companion in Camden, Sea Dog/Bangor features an abundance of made-right-there brews. When we visited in February there were nine, plus Allagash White on the "guest tap." Bar manager Zobeida Peters reported IPA (India Pale Ale) was the best seller. But stout was up there, too. "And," reflected Zobeida, "that's surprising as it's such a heavy drink and it's thick and it doesn't look very good." ('Though, Zobeida admitted, it's one of her favorites.). Sea Dog/Bangor, which is huge, is done up with beer trays/ads, old Bangor photo blowups, and nautical accouterments. The view of the Penobscot River is quite majestic. (Where else can you enjoy a brew and a view of Brewer?). Menu is both "light" (soups, sandwiches, salads) and "heavy" (fish, chicken, steak dinners). For more on Sea Dog/Bangor please see pages 150-151.

Coaster, March 1996

18- SEA DOG BREWPUB, 43 MECHANIC STREET, CAMDEN (11)

"Bewilderment." That's the word Sea Dog employee Tom Abercrombie uses to define how people often feel when they encounter ten made-right-there brews on tap. Some people even get upset... that there's no Bud or Miller. "But," as fellow employee John Griffin points out, "one of the benefits of having so many beers is that there's probably something for everybody." Sea Dog/Camden does, indeed, feature ten of its own brews... all served in an atmosphere chock-a-block with nautical adjuncts and older beer trays/ads. Not to be missed is the view of Megunticook Falls (which appears to flow right through the brewpub!). Menu is hors d'oeuvres, salads, sandwiches, homemade soups, and daily dinner specials. For more on Sea Dog/Camden please see pages 152-153.

There's a host of establishments that score 10... and are thereby tied for slots 19 and 20. These include Benzoni's (Brunswick), Free Street Taverna (Portland), Gritty's (both Freeport and Portland), the Safari (Portland), Stone Coast (Portland), Thirsty Whale (Bar Harbor), and Waterworks (Rockland). We've focused on two: Gritty's/Portland (because it's Maine's pioneer brewpub) and Waterworks (because we just plain like it).

Logo,
March 1996

19- GRITTY McDUFF'S, 396 FORE STREET, PORTLAND (10)

It seems as if Gritty's / Portland has been around forever. But "forever" is 1988. That's the year it opened and what made it so appealing then still makes it appealing now. There's the copper-topped bar, the wainscoting, some neat old beer ads, a lot of brick. Plus, of course, the beer. The day we visited there were eight Maine beers on draught (seven brewed right there; the other from cross-town Geary's). Decor – in addition to the brick and copper et al. – includes a splendid view of Portland Harbor and, sure enough, the brewhouse a level below. Menu is full pub: soups, salads, burgers, plus fish and chips, shepherd's pie, steak & kidney pie, etc. (For more on Gritty's, please see pages 138-139.).

20- WATERWORKS, 7 LINDSEY ST., ROCKLAND (10)

"At first people were amazed to see us open (in March 1995), but then a lot of them said 'Alright, it's about damned time we had a place to go for good quality beer (without having to go to Camden)," laughed Waterworks' owner/manager Susan Barnes the day we stopped by. Waterworks, built into what was a 1930s eight-bay garage, is a gem. There are five Maine beers on draught representing five Maine breweries (Andrew's, Casco Bay, Gritty's, Sheepscot Valley, Shipyard). Decor features a wide-planked floor, dark greens and brick, a giant fieldstone fireplace, a bar made of three strains of mahogany and, in case you get lost, a huge framed 1855 map of Rockland. Menu is upscale pub: soups, salads and sandwiches plus a full nine dinner entrées.

Exterior sign,
March 1996

Artwork by Dick Hubsch, Carmel, N.Y.

WHERE DO WE GO FROM HERE?

Maine has gone from 0 – as in zip – breweries at the midway mark of 1986 to 25 – as in two dozen plus – breweries at the midway mark of 1996. It's a growth rate that can only be termed phenomenal.

The question, of course, is where do we go from here. To get some perspective on that very question I asked the opinion of a trio of people "in the know": Maine brewing pioneer David Geary, Maine brewpub pioneer Richard Pfeffer, and Maine beer savant and author Al Diamon.

David's feeling is that we will continue to see

cont'd. on page 178

It's difficult to fathom just where Maine's next micros/brewpubs might appear. If rumors are to be believed, they could be just about anywhere. And everywhere. Three "futures" that seem to be relatively definite are Bath, Mexico, and The Forks.

In Bath, 40-year old longtime homebrewer Kitridge "Kit" Anderson has high hopes for a brewpub and barbeque restaurant. But Kit, who lives in Bath and works in Brunswick (as a dentist) isn't making any predictions as to when. "Everytime I pick a time," he told me in May, "when I think something might happen... something happens."

Photo, May 1996

This is the Lodge at Northern Outdoors' Resort Center, located at The Forks (also called West Forks; roughly 44 miles north of Skowhegan), as it looked in May 1996. Spread over 100 acres in the upper Kennebec Valley, Northern Outdoors is Maine's oldest and largest outdoor adventure company. When all the adventuring is done, guests have traditionally headed for the Lodge where, until now, they've had to content themselves with a lounge, full-scale restaurant, and, deckside, a sauna and 16-person hot tub. That's all to soon be enhanced, however, by a brewpub. Called the Kennebec River Brewery, the brewpub will have a capacity of 200-300 barrels a year, be located in the basement of the Lodge, feature ales, and be up and operating by October 1996. That's all per Northern Outdoors' prexy Jim Yearwood. Jim, who's 40 and a native of Madawaska, feels the brewpub will nicely "complement" the Lodge's restaurant. But Jim has another interest at stake as well: he's been a home-brewer since 1989. "I like good beer," he told me.

Photo, May 1996

What do you think of when you think of ginseng? An energizing herb? A tea? A mysterious root from the land of the Orient? Well, if Mike DuBois of Mexico has his way, when you think of ginseng in the future you may well think of beer as well. Mike, born in Mexico in 1950, heads up a four-person outfit called Umbagog Trading Company, Inc. Headquarters are in Mexico with branch operations in Dixfield and Andover. A major Umbagog goal is to develop new uses for ginseng, with ginseng/chocolate bars, ginseng/root beer extract and other ginseng goodies already in the fold. Mike was struck with the idea of beer and ginseng while partaking of an ale in the summer of 1994. He's been smitten with the thought since. "It'll be our pièce de résistance," he beams. But will it taste good? Mike thinks so. "I think ginseng will 'balance out' well with hops and malt," he phrases it.

Mike plans to construct a small brewhouse behind Umbagog headquarters on Granite Street in Mexico. He foresees but one blend or brand and he doesn't want to produce very much of it. "I think quantity would take away from quality," he states. Mike's looking at late 1996/early 1997 for first output. His brew, a Belgian-style ale, will be available in bottles in New England and New York. It will be called Father Lafitau, after an early 18th century Jesuit missionary who pioneered the recognition of ginseng in North America.

Stay tuned.

growth (in the number of operating units) for a number of years... although the growth rate will be slow. "But," he laughs, "I say that every year – that the growth rate will be slow – and so far I've been proven wrong." David, incidentally, lumps "shipping breweries" (such as his) with brewpubs, as he feels the category of micros has become "fuzzy," with a trend toward brewpubs doing some packaging for off-premise sales.

Richard looks at the two – shipping and brewpub – separately. He feels there will be few new additions to the shipping pile... but does see a hefty growth for brewpubs. He sees them in "a lot of smaller towns and spread out a little more." Ultimately, however, he sees some consolidation within the ranks; perhaps even one or two "big money players" coming in and setting up a chain or chains.

Al feels that we're "pretty close to maxing out" with respect to shipping micros... but that we "haven't even scratched the surface yet with respect to brewpubs." He visualizes a brewpub in most smaller cities in the state and two or more in the state's larger cities.

My own feelings echo the above. I believe that most every Maine community of any substantial size will enjoy its very own brewpub. In addition to those locales already on line, this would certainly include Augusta, Bath (see previous page), Brunswick, Ellsworth, Lewiston, Rockland, and Waterville. Perhaps Biddeford/ Saco, Damariscotta, Houlton, Kittery, Presque Isle/Caribou, Sanford/Springvale, Waldoboro. (Doug Maffucci of Atlantic Brewing likes to jest that they'll even be a Mars Hill Brewing Company!). And I see this happening before too many more Patriot's Days have passed. I also believe that resort meccas such as Boothbay Harbor, Ogunquit, Old Orchard Beach, and York Beach will have their own brewpubs. And that this, too, shall come to pass before too many more summers have gone by.

But, then again, maybe people will cease enjoying a brew or two and will, instead, develop a passion for egg creams or Moxie or Singapore slings. There's only one thing that's for certain... and that's that, whatever happens, it will be interesting.

A Toast

Here's a toast to you...
And to your good sense.

Beer can make you jump and cheer.
Beer can give you multitudinous kicks.
But beer can also be something to fear...
Because beer and driving in no way mix.

The rhyme is indeed corny.
But the message is not.
DRINKING AND DRIVING DO NOT MIX.
Please do one or please do the other.
But please do **not** do both.

Index